SAP Business Intelligence Quick Start Guide

Actionable business insights from the SAP BusinessObjects
BI platform

Vinay Singh

BIRMINGHAM - MUMBAI

SAP Business Intelligence Quick Start Guide

Commissioning Editor: Amey Varangaonkar
Acquisition Editor: Reshma Raman
Content Development Editor: Kirk Dsouza
Technical Editor: Suwarna Patil
Copy Editor: Safis Editing
Project Coordinator: Hardik Bhinde
Proofreader: Safis Editing
Indexer: Rekha Nair
Graphics: Alishon Mendonsa
Production Coordinator: Jyoti Chauhan

First published: February 2019

Production reference: 1210219

Published by Packt Publishing Ltd.
Livery Place
35 Livery Street
Birmingham
B3 2PB, UK.

ISBN 978-1-78934-620-6

www.packtpub.com

To my daughter Nitara—Life is beautiful with you around.

`mapt.io`

Mapt is an online digital library that gives you full access to over 5,000 books and videos, as well as industry leading tools to help you plan your personal development and advance your career. For more information, please visit our website.

Why subscribe?

- Spend less time learning and more time coding with practical eBooks and Videos from over 4,000 industry professionals

- Improve your learning with Skill Plans built especially for you

- Get a free eBook or video every month

- Mapt is fully searchable

- Copy and paste, print, and bookmark content

Packt.com

Did you know that Packt offers eBook versions of every book published, with PDF and ePub files available? You can upgrade to the eBook version at `www.packt.com` and as a print book customer, you are entitled to a discount on the eBook copy. Get in touch with us at `customercare@packtpub.com` for more details.

At `www.packt.com`, you can also read a collection of free technical articles, sign up for a range of free newsletters, and receive exclusive discounts and offers on Packt books and eBooks.

Contributors

About the author

Vinay Singh is a data science manager at BASF, Germany. He has over 12 years' experience in data warehousing and BI. Before joining BASF, he worked with multiple companies/customers, including SAP, Adobe Systems, Freudenberg, and T-Systems, which provided him with a good mix of product development and consulting experience.

His other publications include *Real-Time Analytics with SAP HANA*, published by *Packt*, *Manage Your SAP Projects with SAP Activate*, also published by Packt, and *Creating and Using Advanced DSOs in SAP BW on SAP HANA*, by *SAP PRESS*. He is a visiting research scholar at the National Central University of Taiwan, and a distinguished speaker at various forums.

I would firstly like to thank my wife, Minal, for her understanding of the time I spent on this book and for her regular feedback. I would also like to thank Prof. Dr. Shiuann-Shuoh Chen, for his encouragement and support in allowing me to work with student groups from the ERP center, National Central University of Taiwan. Finally, I would like to thank all the editors of this book, with special thanks going to Kirk Dsouza.

About the reviewer

Parag Terwadkar has extensive experience (over 12 years) in the IT industry and has worked in multiple technologies throughout his career, starting with SAP R/3 through to big data. He has spent several years working closely with clients, and currently works for Accenture GmbH in a managerial role.

He is also a FIDE rated chess player and loves spending lots of time participating in, and following, all kinds of sports.

Packt is searching for authors like you

If you're interested in becoming an author for Packt, please visit `authors.packtpub.com` and apply today. We have worked with thousands of developers and tech professionals, just like you, to help them share their insight with the global tech community. You can make a general application, apply for a specific hot topic that we are recruiting an author for, or submit your own idea.

Table of Contents

Preface

This book will serve as an introduction to the SAP BusinessObjects BI platform, and will introduce readers to the different data visualization, visual analytics, reporting, and dashboarding capabilities of the tool.

Who this book is for

BI professionals and existing SAP ecosystem users who wish to perform effective BI using SAP BusinessObjects will benefit from this book. It will serve as an introduction to the SAP BusinessObjects BI platform. By the end of this book, readers will be comfortable in using the SAP BusinessObjects tool for all their needs pertaining to BI for effective strategizing/decision making.

What this book covers

Chapter 1, *Overview of SAP BusinessObject Business Intelligence 4.2*, provides a high-level overview of SAP BusinessObjects BI 4.2. We will walk through SAP BI solutions and its benefits, identifying the components of SAP BusinessObjects 4.2 and enterprise data sources for SAP BI reporting tools.

Chapter 2, *SAP BusinessObject Analysis*, explains how to create a basic workbook with SAP BusinessObjects Analysis (Microsoft Office edition). We will also see how to manage SAP NetWeaver BW and SAP HANA data sources for Microsoft Office functionality.

Chapter 3, *SAP BusinessObject Design Studio*, explains SAP BusinessObjects Design Studio and walks the reader through various concepts related to Design Studio, namely, initial view, layout, and architecture.

Chapter 4, *SAP BusinessObject Web Intelligence*, describes how to create an SAP BusinessObjects Web Intelligence document and how to use features such as query, report, and analyze with SAP BusinessObjects Web Intelligence (Webi)

Chapter 5, *SAP BusinessObject Crystal Reports*, describes how to create a report in SAP Crystal Report for Enterprise and explores the variety of toolbars and report elements that are available.

Chapter 6, *SAP BusinessObject SAP Lumira*, provides a general overview of SAP Lumira. We will learn how to visualize and manipulate data using an SAP Lumira storyboard.

Chapter 7, *SAP BusinessObject Predictive Analytics 2.0*, covers how to use SAP predictive analytics and explains how the SAP predictive analytics toolset can be used.

Chapter 8, *BI Platform Features*, explains how to use SAP predictive analytics, with a focus on data mining.

Chapter 9, *BI Platform Deployment*, provides a general overview of the SAP BusinessObjects BI platform architecture, BI systems, and the elements contained within BI systems.

To get the most out of this book

You should have some basic knowledge of SAP and BI. Even though we will be discussing SAP BusinessObjects BI from scratch, some prior knowledge of SAP is always beneficial.

You will require access to SAP BusinessObjects systems. You may even acquire an Amazon Web Service / Microsoft Azure subscription for the BusinessObjects system required.

At the end of each chapter, there are exercises, with screenshots demonstrating how to carry them out. Please complete these exercises and also complete the activities that the author has set as learning exercises for readers.

Download the color images

We also provide a PDF file that has color images of the screenshots/diagrams used in this book. You can download it here:
http://www.packtpub.com/sites/default/files/downloads/9781789346206_ColorImages.pdf.

Conventions used

There are a number of text conventions used throughout this book.

CodeInText: Indicates code words in text, database table names, folder names, filenames, file extensions, pathnames, dummy URLs, user input, and Twitter handles. Here is an example: "Open the IDT and create a new project called UNI_relational_data as follows."

Bold: Indicates a new term, an important word, or words that you see on screen. For example, words in menus or dialog boxes appear in the text like this. Here is an example: "Click on **Information Design Tool**."

 Warnings or important notes appear like this.

 Tips and tricks appear like this.

Get in touch

Feedback from our readers is always welcome.

General feedback: If you have questions about any aspect of this book, mention the book title in the subject of your message and email us at customercare@packtpub.com.

Errata: Although we have taken every care to ensure the accuracy of our content, mistakes do happen. If you have found a mistake in this book, we would be grateful if you would report this to us. Please visit www.packt.com/submit-errata, selecting your book, clicking on the Errata Submission Form link, and entering the details.

Piracy: If you come across any illegal copies of our works in any form on the internet, we would be grateful if you would provide us with the location address or website name. Please contact us at copyright@packt.com with a link to the material.

If you are interested in becoming an author: If there is a topic that you have expertise in, and you are interested in either writing or contributing to a book, please visit authors.packtpub.com.

Reviews

Please leave a review. Once you have read and used this book, why not leave a review on the site that you purchased it from? Potential readers can then see and use your unbiased opinion to make purchase decisions, we at Packt can understand what you think about our products, and our authors can see your feedback on their book. Thank you!

For more information about Packt, please visit packt.com.

Section 1: Introduction to SAP Business Intelligence

This section serves as an introduction to SAP BusinessObjects Business Intelligence 4.2, where we will set the tone for the book. It contains one chapter, covering an overview of the BI platform and various data sources for reporting purposes. This section contains only one chapter which is Chapter 1, *Overview of SAP BusinessObjects Business Intelligence 4.2*.

1
Overview of SAP BusinessObject Business Intelligence 4.2

This book will take you through the concepts related to SAP **Business Intelligence** (**BI**) and the tools associated with the SAP BusinessObjects BI platform 4.2. While we start with basic concepts and understanding the platform, and gradually progress to deeper insights into the various tools offered by the platform. The book offers a good overview of all the tools with examples of how to use the functionalities offered by each tool.

This chapter provides a high-level overview of SAP BusinessObjects BI 4.2. We will walk through SAP BusinessObjects BI 4.2 and its benefits, identifying the components of SAP BusinessObjects BI 4.2 and enterprise data sources for BI reporting tools. We will learn about the SAP BusinessObjects BI platform and different BI tools that are available to use in a business scenario. We will learn how to create a **Business Explorer** (**BEx**) query to directly access SAP BW as data source. We will use these data sources, connections, and business layers in upcoming chapters.

In this chapter, we will cover the following topics:

- BI and its benefits
- Components of SAP BusinessObjects 4.2
- Enterprise data sources for BI reporting tools
- Creating a BEx query to directly access SAP BW as data source
- Local data sources

BI and its benefits

BI is a strategic and reporting tool with sets of methodologies and processes for transforming data into meaningful insights, such as sales reports, slice and dice finance reports, and predictive analysis, to support decision making.

Some of the benefits are as follows:

- Decreased query and reporting time
- Identifying and track key performance metrics against their direct competitors and the overall market
- It is fast at providing reports, performing analysis, and planning
- It helps you make better business decisions
- It directly helps to reduce costs, which leads to higher revenue for an organization

The SAP BusinessObjects BI platform provides an enterprise BI with systems that are scalable, flexible, and adaptive. They have a **service-oriented architecture (SOA)** that allows us to deploy and standardize SAP BusinessObjects BI implementations. SAP offers both a suite of reporting tools with a full spectrum of features and a new cloud solution as a so-called **software-as-a-service (SaaS)** offering. In this book, we will discuss the traditional SAP BusinessObjects tools and the new predictive analytics tools. With SAP BI, you can get insights in the following areas:

- **Data discovery**: With SAP BusinessObjects you can discover, analyze, and share. It can do the following:
    - Mash up data from multiple sources
    - Create visualizations
    - Combine visualizations to tell a story
- **Applications and dashboards**: It enables you to build engaging experience in the following ways:
    - It allows you to create dynamic and customizable applications and dashboards
    - You can engage in sophisticated planning and predictive applications out-of-the-box
    - It's capable of delivering engaging information to users where they need it

- **Reporting**: You can distribute formatted information:
  - Securely distribute information across the organization
  - Create interactive reports
  - Create personalized reports via email

Components of SAP BusinessObjects 4.2

SAP BusinessObject BI platform 4.2 is a reporting and analytics platform that targets business users. It is an innovation platform that simplifies, enhances, and extends the capabilities of BI. It consists of a number of reporting applications with which a user can discover data, create applications and dashboards, and perform analytics to derive business insights. The platform ensures increased responsiveness, reduced costs and workload, and helps organizations to make better decisions.

We need to understand the various tools available in SAP BusinessObject 4.2 to perform reporting. There are multiple management tools, platform services, and client tools in SAP BusinessObjects 4.2 that support the entire range of user reporting, queries, analysis, and performance management.

Some of the salient features of the SAP BI platform are as follows:

- BI content management allows the secure storage of BI content
- It provides a software development kit, which can be used by the API to extend the solution or for making the process automated
- It is possible to distribute personalized BI content to a large audience in an automated manner
- It gives the ability to scale up and scale out to suit growing demand
- It provides services to the audit trail for compliance or capacity planning

The following diagram shows the overview of the architecture of SAP BusinessObjects BI:

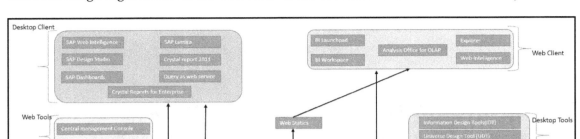

The following are some of the main BusinessObjects BI platforms:

- **Central Management Console (CMC)**
- **Server Intelligence Agent (SIA)**
- **Central Configuration Manager (CCM)**
- **Central Management Servers (CMS)**
- Semantic layer tool
- Client tools

In the next section, let's examine in detail the following platform tools for administration:

- **CMC**
- **CCM**
- **Lifecycle Management (LCM)** tools

Central Management Console

In SAP BusinessObjects BI, the CMC is the main web interface used to perform any administrative task, which also includes managing servers. It also allows us to publish and organize content, transfer BI platform objects across our SAP BusinessObjects BI platform landscape, and configure security settings. As the CMC is a web-based application, we can perform all the administrative tasks in a web browser on any computer that can connect to the web application server. All users can log on to the CMC to change their own preference settings. Only members of the administrators group can change management settings, unless a user is explicitly granted rights to do so. Roles can be assigned in the CMC to grant user privileges to perform minor administrative tasks, such as managing users in your group and managing reports in folders that belong to your team.

> The CMC is a web-based application that allows and enables you to do administrative tasks remotely.

Central Configuration Manager

CCM is tool that's used to view and modify server settings when the SAP BusinessObjects server processes are offline. It is widely used to create and configure nodes and to start and stop the web application server. Another very important usage of CCM is to configure the SIA and to start or stop the server. It can operate in both Unix and Microsoft Windows environments.

In a Unix environment, the shell script allows us to manage servers from the command line, and in Microsoft Windows we get a graphical user interface. The Microsoft Windows environment allows us to makes network parameter changes in one go to all servers within a node.

> Many users use CCM for troubleshooting and node configuration. For other administrative tasks, CMC is preferred.

Lifecycle Management

The LCM console is a web-based tool (within CMC) that allows the management of different versions of BI resources, dependencies, and a mechanism to roll back to a previous state. The LCM console is a standard functionality with the standard installation of SAP BusinessObjects BI. It helps administrators and developers to package their developments in transportable groups of objects and detects the dependencies of objects that need to be transported to other objects, which aren't manually added to the transport. The console comes as both a web interface and as a command-line tool and comes with a wide range of functionality to support the tasks related to software management. It establishes procedures for governing the entire life cycle of an object within the scope of the BI platform. If an object needs other objects to work correctly in the target environment, LCM allows it to analyze which other objects are necessary to make the object work in the destination. This functionality offers a considerable improvement in both speed and quality, compared to a manual object collection process. Several objects are gathered in a definition of a promotion job, which includes not only what is transported, but also when and where the objects are transported.

To manage complex implementations of SAP BusinessObjects BI, it is necessary to implement a solution for the LCM of the objects created and managed in SAP BusinessObjects BI. There are three phases in LCM—**development**, **testing**, and **production**. Examples of LCM objects are SAP Crystal Reports documents, folders, connections, and Universe.

Enterprise data sources for BI reporting tools

There are many data source options for SAP BusinessObjects 4.2. You can get data for reporting from nearly all possible real-world sources. In the following diagram, there is a typical scenario for data sources for SAP BusinessObjects 4.2:

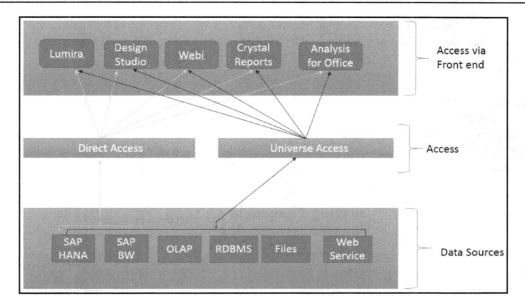

In this book, we will focus on the following important data sources:

- SAP HANA
- SAP **Business Warehouse (BW)**
- SAP BusinessObjects Universe
- Files

> In general, Universe and semantic layers are used interchangeably. Both are common business terms meaning a collection of corporate data. In our case, in addition to Universe, SAP HANA views and SAP BW queries also qualify as semantic layers.

A semantic layer in SAP BusinessObjects BI enables the following:

- A single user experience across all data
- Consistency
- Ease of consumption by applications and tools
- Business user, who is self-sufficient

Semantic layers in SAP BusinessObjects are represented by Universe objects that are created with the **Information Design Tool** (**IDT**) and stored in the SAP BusinessObjects BI platform repository.

Most reporting tools have access to a wide range of data sources. There are regular updates to the reporting tools, so consult the official documentation for each tool in the release you are deploying. Some of these tools let users prepare data, and others add the ability to merge data from different sources. Here is a table detailing the abilities of these tools:

Tools	Data merging and prep	Universe access (multiple underlying sources)	SAP BW	SAP HANA	File
SAP Lumira—desktop	Yes	Yes	Yes	Yes	Yes (CSV and XLS)
Analysis Office—Excel and PowerPoint add-in	Yes	No	Yes	Yes	Yes (using native Excel features)
Design Studio—desktop and browser	No	Yes	Yes	Yes	Yes (local mode only)
Web Intelligence	Yes	Yes	Yes	Yes	Yes
Crystal Reports Enterprise	Yes	Yes	Yes	Yes	Yes

By leveraging the Universe as a **Common Semantic Layer** (**CSL**), you can enable a consistent business user experience. CSL allows heterogeneous access to all data sources (for example, OLAP and relational databases) and supports native metadata such as OLAP hierarchies.

 In most cases, direct access (via **Business Intelligence Consumer Services** (**BICS**)) to SAP HANA and SAP BW is the preferred option.

Information Design Tool

The IDT is a tool that's used to build the Universe of fields that are used by end users to build reports.

These are the features of IDT:

- A single development environment for building Universes against relational, dimensional, and multi-source data sources
- Clear separation between the data foundation and the business layer
- Share the work with a team of designers
- Manage security when you make new interfaces
- Preview data results as you develop you project

There are many underlying sources of data that can be accessed through a Universe. They include the following:

- SAP BW
- Microsoft **Structured Query Language (SQL)** server
- Oracle
- IBM DB2
- IBM Netezza
- SAP IQ
- Teradata

Creating a Universe with the IDT

Let's see how to create a Universe with the IDT. In this exercise, we will create a Universe as a semantic layer on top of a database. This Universe then later can be consumed via Web Intelligence users to report on key sales figures.

Getting started with the tool

Open the IDT and create a new project called `UNI_relational_data` as follows:

1. Click on **Information Design Tool**.
2. Choose **File** | **New** | **Project**:

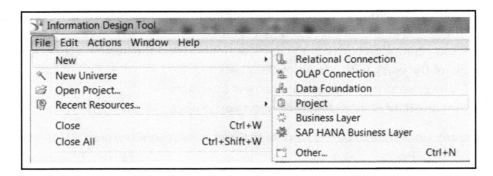

3. Enter `UNI_relational_data` (or any name) as the project name and choose **Finish**. The following screenshot shows you the summary of the preceding steps (creating a project in IDT):

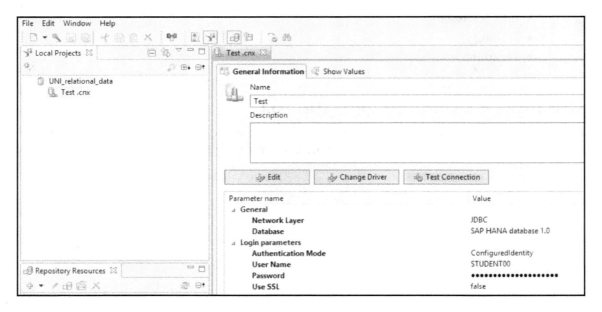

Use the user credentials and other details based on database used (here I am using a SAP HANA database). This information is available from your system administrator.

Creating a new relational connection

Create a new relational connection in your local project. Since I am using a SAP HANA database in my example, I will create it in a HANA database. You can choose a different database if you want:

1. Choose the project we just created (UNI_relational_data) and choose **File | New | Relational Connection**
2. Enter UNI_eFashion as the source name and add description of your own and choose **Next**
3. Choose **SAP HANA database 1.0 | JDBC Drivers** and choose **Next**
4. Fill in the required credentials and choose **Finish**
5. Choose **Test Connection** to verify that the connection works

6. Create a data source (**Relational data source**):

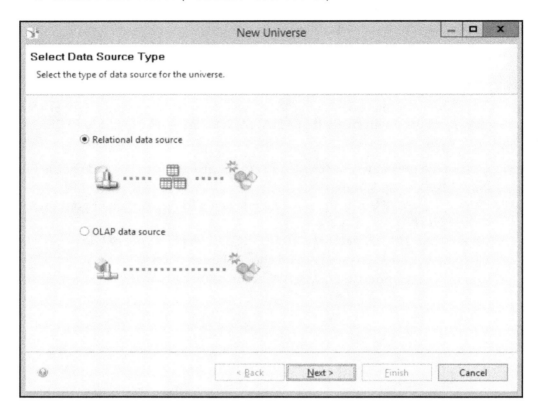

7. Choose the database and the driver (here, I chose **SAP HANA** and **JDBC Drivers**):

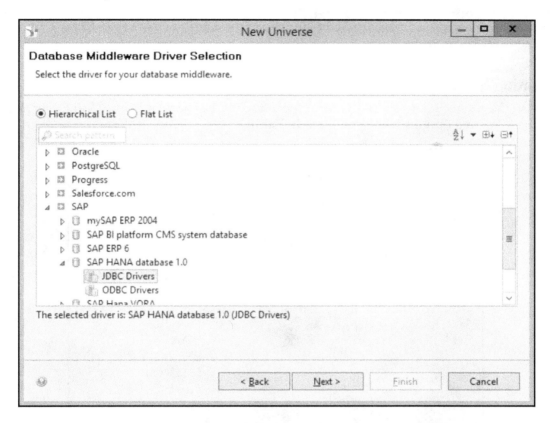

Before we proceed further, let's try to understand the difference between the local connection and the repository connection. In IDT, a connection can be used to connect to a relational or an OLAP data source using the SAP BusinessObjects reporting tool. It can be a local connection or a connection that is published in a central repository. Any user running IDT can access a local connection. It becomes a secured connection when we publish the connection to the repository.

A .cnx extension in the connection shows that it is a local connection. It does not mean that it is a shortcut present to the secured connection from the SAP BusinessObjects repository. You are not allowed to publish anything in the repository if you use this connection. .cns is the extension shortcut that is linked to the secured connection from the SAP BusinessObjects repository.

Creating a shortcut in our local folder

Publish the connection to the BI platform repository and a shortcut in our local folder. You get the following options when you want to **Publish**:

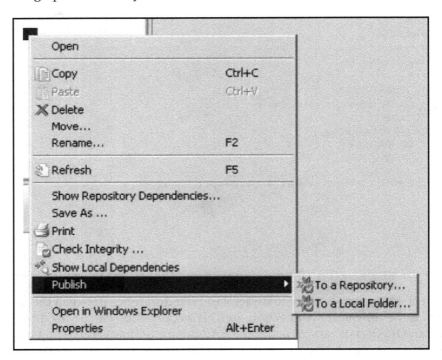

Now, let's come back to our exercise and create a shortcut in our local folder:

1. Select UNI_eFashion.cnx (created earlier) connection to a repository
2. Choose **File | Publish | Publish Connection to a Repository**:

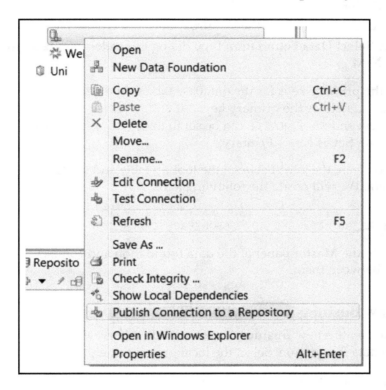

3. Enter the credentials and choose to **connect**
4. Click on **Connection folder | Insert folder | Finish**
5. Choose **Yes**, and the shortcut will be created

Tutorial tables from SAP are available for download at https://wiki.scn.sap.com/wiki/display/BOBJ/eFashion+on+HANA.

Creating a single source data foundation

Create a single source data foundation called UNI_eFashion, based on the secured version of the relational connection (.cns).

Include the ARTICLE_LOOKUP, CALENDER_YEAR_LOOKUP, and SHOP_FACTS tables (download the tables from the preceding link):

1. Select the UNI_relational_data project and choose **File | New Data Foundation**
2. Enter UNI_eFashion as the resource name and choose **Next**
3. In the **Select Data Foundation** type dialog box, select **single source radio** and then **Next**

We need to set the primary keys for the database tables. In the ARTICLE_LOOKUP table, we set the ARTICLE_ID field as the primary key; CALENDER_YEAR_LOOKUP will have WEEK_ID as the primary key; and SHOP_FACTS can be set to SHOP_FACTS_ID by right-clicking on the fields and choosing **Set as Key | Primary**.

Then we need to create the joins between the lookup table and the fact table with the transactional data. We will create the following joins:

```
ARTICLE_LOOKUP.ARTICLE_ID  |  SHOP_FACTS.ARTICLE_ID
CALENDAR_YEAR_LOOKUP.WEEK_ID  |  SHOP_FACTS.WEEK_ID
```

To do so, we go to the **Master** panel of the data foundation and connect the fields by dragging a line between them.

Creating a new Business Layer with a file

Now we need to create a new **Business Layer** with the filename UNI_eFashion for the UNI_eFashion data foundation. Select the local project folder, UNI_relational_data:

1. Choose **File | New | Business Layer**:

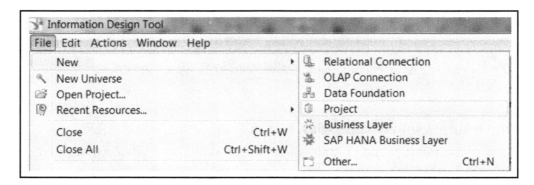

2. Select **Relational Data Foundation** and choose **Next**:

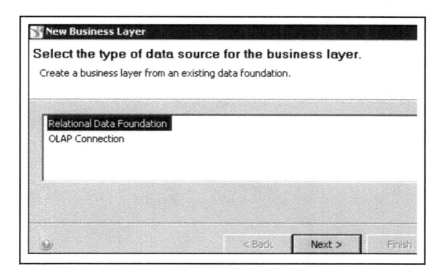

3. Enter `UNI_eFashion` as **Resource name** and choose **Next**.
4. Choose the `UNI_eFashion` data foundation. Deselect **Automatically create class and objects for SAP HANA connection** checkbox.
5. Choose **Finish**.
6. In the **Business Layer** panel, choose `UNI_eFashion` and choose the arrow next to the **Insert Object** button:

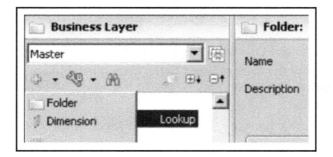

7. Choose **Folder**.

8. In the **Name** field, we will enter **Article Date** and repeat the previous steps for **Measure** and **Dimension**.
9. We can then add the objects to folders.

Creating a query on the Business Layer using Query Panel

Now, on the **Business Layer** defined previously we can create a query using **Query Panel**, and then execute it. We can do this by following these steps:

1. Choose **Queries** on the **Business Layer** panel:

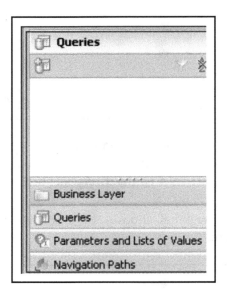

2. Click on the **Insert Query** button to open **Query Panel**
3. Expand each of the folders listed in the previous table and drag the corresponding dimension and measures to **Result Objects** for **Query Panel**
4. Choose **OK**
5. Now execute the query by clicking on the **Execute Query** button

Publish the **Business Layer** as a Universe to the BI platform repository:

1. Choose the `UNI_relational_data` project **File** I **Save All**
2. Right-click `UNI_eFashion` and choose **Publish** I **To a Repository**
3. Choose **Check all**, click on the **Check Integrity** button, and click **Next**
4. Choose **Finish**

We just created a Universe with the IDT that accesses a SAP HANA database. The same can be done for all other data sources. As discussed earlier, data sources (SAP HANA and SAP BW) can be directly accessed without using a Universe. By following these steps to directly access the data sources (SAP BW and SAP HANA), the readers create their own, as a kind of assignment for this chapter.

Creating a BEx query to directly access SAP BW as a data source

You can again use the sample data from eFashion that we have downloaded earlier. We will refer the dataset from eFashion, you can choose cube of your own that is available in your system:

1. Start BEx Query Designer and connect to the SAP BW system when asked to provide login credentials.
2. Create a new BEx Query using the **Info Provider eFashion** cube. Move the characteristic store (`technical name = EF_STORE`) to the **Rows** section.
3. Use the basic key figures, amount sold (`EFAMTSOLD`) and quantity sold (`QTY_SOLD`), in the **Columns** section.
4. Save the query in the `role` folder.
5. Execute the query in the BEx Web Analyzer to view the data and see if it is correct.
6. Make the necessary changes in the BEx query definition to enable users of your report.
7. To select the data related to specific countries states (`EF_STATE`). Save the query and execute it in BEx Web Analyzer in the same way you did previously.
8. Execute the report with restrictions on `STATE` and check the results.

Displaying the SAP HANA view using the SAP HANA live browser

To use SAP HANA models directly via web-based browser we need to follow these steps. Before starting, please finalize the query that you want to view. Here, I am using `MaterialValuatedStockQuery`:

1. Log on to **SAP HANA Live Explorer** by using the following URL and your SAP HANA credentials: `http://<sap hana server hostname >:8000/sap/hba/explorer/`.
2. Your SAP Basis colleagues will provide the **SAP HANA Server Hostname**.
3. Use **Application Component** view to locate the query.
4. View the structure of the query and business data.
5. Display the related view and the tables from where the data is sourced. Then **show all**, show the dependencies as a graph.
6. Add the view to your favorites so it is easy to locate next time.
7. Select the views in the **HANA** tab and repeat the preceding steps using the **efashion/CALC_AN_SALES** view.

Local data sources

Files, although normally not the optimal choice, can be used to directly feed the reporting tools and Universes. Most reporting tools can directly access file sources, such as CSV and XLS file types. In addition, Universes can get data from files and then feed the reporting tool indirectly.

We have seen many customers use this option in combination with other data sources (such as DW, SAP HANA). A typical use cases is reading the actual sales figures from data mart, whereas the target values are read from spreadsheets.

What is the prerequisite for installing SAP HANA Live?
You need SAP HANA Appliance Software Support Package Stack 08 or higher, or SAP HANA Studio Software Support Package Stack 08 or higher. You can use the **Software Update Manager** (**SUM**) for SAP HANA to catch up with the recent updates if SAP HANA Appliance software is already installed.

Summary

With this chapter, we laid the foundations for the book. The intention was to quickly go through the basic concepts and refresh users who are already familiar with SAP BusinessObjects BI 4.2. By now, we should have learned the basics of BusinessObjects 4.2 and the different tools available to use in a business scenario. We also learned how to access various data sources with and without a SAP BusinessObject Universe. We will use these data sources, connections, and business layers in the upcoming chapters.

In the next chapter, we will learn how to create a basic workbook with SAP BusinessObjects Analysis for Microsoft Office, followed by creating a presentation using BusinessObjects Analysis for Microsoft PowerPoint.

Section 2: Data Visualization, Analysis, and Reporting

This section focuses on data visualization, analysis, reporting, and analytics with BusinessObjects BI tools. You'll learn how to create interactive data visualizations and analyze them with the various tools available under the portfolio of SAP BusinessObjects. This section has six chapters in total.

The following chapters are included in this section:

- Chapter 2, *SAP BusinessObject Analysis*
- Chapter 3, *SAP BusinessObject Design Studio*
- Chapter 4, *SAP BusinessObject Web Intelligence*
- Chapter 5, *SAP BusinessObject Crystal Reports*
- Chapter 6, *SAP BusinessObject SAP Lumira*
- Chapter 7, *SAP BusinessObject Predictive Analytics 2.0*

SAP BusinessObject Analysis 2

In this chapter, we'll learn how to create a basic workbook with SAP BusinessObjects Analysis for Microsoft Office. This will help us learn how to use BEx query elements in the SAP BusinessObjects Analysis edition for Microsoft Office. We will create a report on a BEx query to analyze our SAP BW data. We'll also see how to manage SAP NetWeaver **Business Warehouse** (**BW**) and SAP HANA data sources for Microsoft Office functionality. We will also try our hands with direct access to SAP HANA views and display and analyze the data in SAP BusinessObjects Analysis edition for Microsoft Office.

After completing this chapter, you should be familiar with the functionality of SAP BusinessObjects Analysis editions for Microsoft and **Online Analytical Processing** (**OLAP**). We'll conclude this chapter by creating a live Microsoft PowerPoint presentation.

We'll learn about the following topics and the concepts related to them:

- SAP BusinessObjects Analysis for Microsoft
- Creating a basic workbook with SAP BusinessObjects Analysis for Microsoft
- Creating a presentation using BusinessObjects Analysis for Microsoft PowerPoint

Introduction to SAP BusinessObjects Analysis for Microsoft

SAP BusinessObjects Analysis for Microsoft Office allows ad hoc multidimensional analysis of OLAP sources in Microsoft Excel, creating and embedding intuitive BI into live Microsoft PowerPoint presentations, and Microsoft Excel workbook-based application design. If you're acquainted with using SAP BEx, SAP BusinessObjects Analysis for Microsoft Office is the premium alternative and eventual replacement to the SAP BEx analyzer.

In Microsoft Excel, Analysis is available as a separate tab in the ribbon. The ribbon is part of the Microsoft Office user interface that's above the main work area that presents commands and options. Some analysis options are available in the ribbon tab under **Analysis** in MS Excel.

Using SAP BusinessObjects Analysis for Microsoft, we can perform the following tasks:

- Analyze and interact with data in Microsoft Excel
- Create predefined workbooks
- Create a live data presentation using Microsoft PowerPoint

The following diagram displays the data connectivity in SAP BusinessObjects Analysis for Microsoft Office:

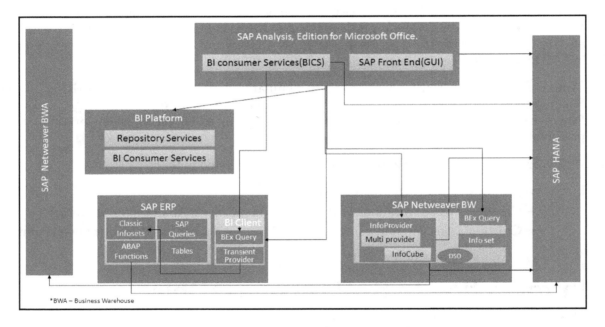

As shown in the preceding architectural function diagram, SAP Analysis edition for Microsoft Office can be connected in the following ways as follows:

- Directly to SAP NetWeaver BW through SAP BusinessObjects **BI Consumer Services (BICS)**
- Connection management through the SAP BusinessObjects BI platform (optional)
- SAP BusinessObjects BI platform repository services for Microsoft Excel and Microsoft PowerPoint

In SAP BusinessObjects Analysis 1.3 and above, we can save SAP Analysis workbooks to the SAP NetWeaver platform without using the SAP BusinessObjects BI platform. To do that, we have to change the preferred platform settings in SAP that is BusinessObjects Analysis to NetWeaver (save workbooks in the SAP NetWeaver platform only) or to **Selectable** (choose if you want to save workbooks in BI or NetWeaver platform).

It has the following target groups and typical use case:

Target group	Use cases
Business users	They are consumers of predefined BI content in Microsoft Excel and PowerPoint.
Business analysts	Ad hoc data access, data analysis, and slice and dice of data in Microsoft Excel and embedding of BI data into PowerPoint presentation IT and superuser creation of SAP BusinessObjects Analysis content.
IT and superusers	Creates content. This content iscentrally created so that it can be pushed to all the business users and business analysts. They are also responsible for workbook design.

A basic workbook with SAP BusinessObjects Analysis for Microsoft

A SAP BusinessObjects Analysis workbook makes it possible for users to filter and manipulate data. It enables us to recognize trends and differences within Excel. The focus here is to enable business analysts and business users to prepare such reports on their own without the support of an IT department. SAP BusinessObjects Analysis is present as a separate tab in Microsoft Excel.

The following diagram gives an overview of the **Analysis** tab in Excel:

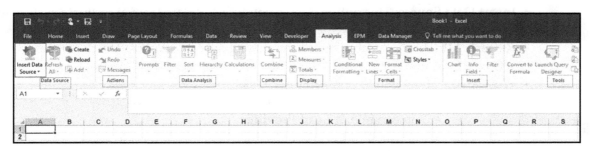

Overview of the Analysis tab in Excel

It consists of the following groups:

- **Data Source**
- **Actions**
- **Data Analysis**
- **Combine**
- **Display**
- **Format**
- **Insert**
- **Tools**
- **Planning**
- **Design Panel**

The list of groups

Let's try to go through some of the groups in detail, as follows:

- The **Data Source** group
- The **Data Analysis** group
- The **Combine** and **Display** group
- The **Insert** and **Tools** group

The Data Source group

This group consists of tabs related to a data source that can act as a source. It consists of the following options that you can choose from:

- **Insert Data Source**: This option allows you to insert data from any source system into a crosstab.
- **Refresh All**: This is mostly used for refreshing all data sources. The data from the server gets updated correspondingly and the crosstab gets redrawn.
- Workspaces allow you to perform three tasks:
  - You can use this option to create **Local Provider**
  - You can reload **Load Provider**
  - You can add **Local Provider** to the data source and create **Composite Provider**

The Data Analysis group

This group consists of tabs that can be used to analyze data. It consists of the following options:

- **Prompts**: You can input the query parameters and variables values here. The crosstab will then display according to the selected values.
- **Filter**: Data can be filtered by measure or by member.
- **Sort**: It's possible to sort the date to visualize and organize the data in the crosstab with different views.
- **Hierarchy**: The hierarchy options, such as expansion level and parent member positions, can be defined here.
- **Calculations**: You can define your calculations here; they can either be simple calculations or dynamic.

The Combine and Display groups

With the tabs in the **Combine** group, you can use the group crosstabs or link dimensions.

The **Display** group consists of the following options to configure and control the display:

- `Members`: This is used for configuring display for members based on key or text
- `Measures`: With this, we can define the display options for measures such as decimal places and scaling factor
- `Totals`: This is used for configuring the display, position, and calculation of total

The Insert and Tools groups

The **Insert** group contains various visualization options such as **Chart**, **Info Field**, and **Filter**:

- **Chart**: This feature allows you to enable/insert dynamic charts
- **Info Field**: Basic information such as name can be inserted through this tab
- **Filter**: This tab is useful for simple data filtering.

 Dynamic charts—these are charts that gets updated dynamically. The key is to define the chart's source data as a dynamic range. By doing so, the chart will automatically reflect changes and additions to the source data.

The **Tools** group contains a collection of tools such as **Smart Copy, Smart Paste**, and **Convert to Formula**, which can act as shortcuts and come in handy for frequent tasks:

- **Convert to Formula**: This is used for extracting Excel formulas after they have been converted from the crosstab to fetch data
- **Smart Copy**: This field can be used to copy data from the clipboard
- **Smart Paste**: This tab allows you to paste the data source from the clipboard as a table
- **Save View**: A data source can be saved as a view using this option

Creating a SAP BusinessObjects Analysis workbook

Now, let's learn how to create a SAP BusinessObjects Analysis workbook based on an existing SAP HANA calculation view. You can use an existing BEx query as well instead of a SAP HANA calculation view.

Here, I'll show the step-by-step procedure of creating a workbook using an existing SAP HANA calculation view and then I'll explain how to do it with a BEx query.

Follow these steps (we'll use the eFashion dataset and HANA view that we used in Chapter 1, *Overview of SAP BusinessObject Business Intelligence 4.2*. You can also refer to this link for more information on eFashion: https://wiki.scn.sap.com/wiki/display/BOBJ/eFashion+on+HANA

1. Start SAP BusinessObjects Analysis, the Microsoft Excel edition, and then, in the options, mark **Preferred Platform** as **Selectable**. This will allow us to choose either NetWeaver or the BI platform so that we can save our workbooks:
    1. Click on the Windows key on your keyboard and, on the top-right of your screen, search for **Analysis for Microsoft Excel**
    2. Create a new worksheet based on a blank template
    3. If the **Preferred Platform** setting isn't set to **Selectable**, then choose **File** and then **Setting** and select the **Preferred Platform** option and change it to **Selectable**

2. Insert the SAP HANA calculation view, AN_SALES, starting at cell **A1**:
   1. Click on **Analysis | Insert | Select Data Source**.
   2. It will ask for SAP BusinessObjects BI platform credentials; enter the details and log on, as displayed here:

   3. In the **Select Data Source** dialog box, set **Show Connections** to **All** and double-click the **HANA_HTTP** connection. Then, enter the necessary credentials, as displayed here:

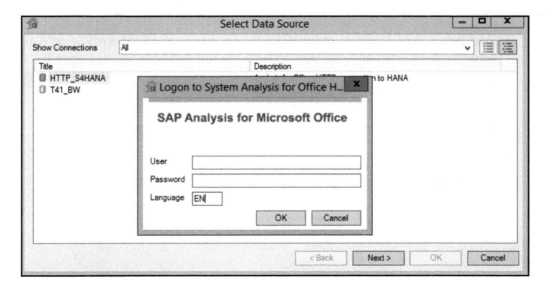

4. Choose the **Area** tab and select the cube radio button; expand the eFashion folder and double-click the view AN_SALES.

5. The query results are displayed in cell **A1**. However, the view includes all Measures and no attributes:

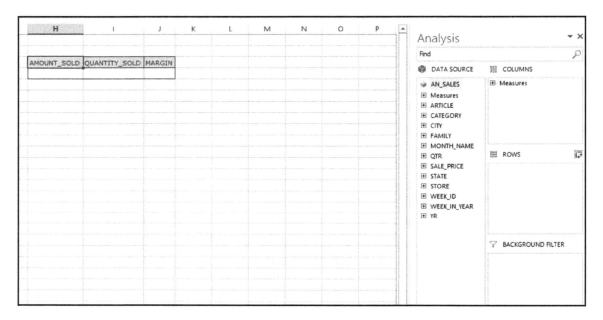

3. As there was no attribute in the default layout from the SAP HANA view, we'll add STATE, STORE, and CATEGORY (keep the same order):

1. Drag the STATE, STORE, and CATEGORY attributes from the **DATA SOURCE** pane into the **ROWS** pane:

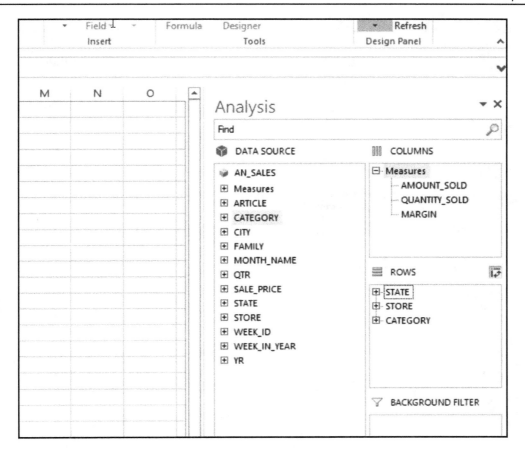

2. Select the cell containing the words: **Store in the body of the workbook**. Drag this to the left of the STATE cell to swap **COLUMNS**.

4. Remove all of `Measures` from the reports and just keep `AMOUNT_SOLD` and `QUALITY_SOLD`:

  1. In the **COLUMNS** panel, select the `Measures` node and then right-click on `COLOUR_CODE` and select **Remove**:

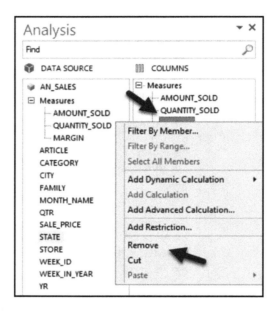

  2. Follow the same steps to remove all of the other `Measures`
  3. Drag `AMOUNT_SOLD` under `QUALITY_SOLD` to change the order of `Measures`:

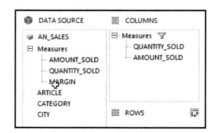

5. Restore the initial order of `Measures` and characteristics:

  1. Before we complete this step, we need to make sure that the report isn't getting refreshed after each action, so we need to choose **Pause Refresh** in the **Analysis** tab.

2. In the `Measures` panel, change the order of the measure again. Make sure that the display in the spreadsheet doesn't change.

3. In the **ROWS** panel, change the order of `STATE | STORE`. Again, make sure the display in the spreadsheet doesn't change.

4. Choose **Pause Refresh** again.

5. All changes should be reflected in the spreadsheet.

6. Remove the `STORE` attribute from **ROWS** and define the filters setting for `STATE` as follows:

    1. Display `California` and `Florida`:

    2. In the **ROWS** panel, right-click the `STORE` attribute and choose **Remove**.

    3. In **Analysis**, go to **A1 | Filter | Filter By Member**:

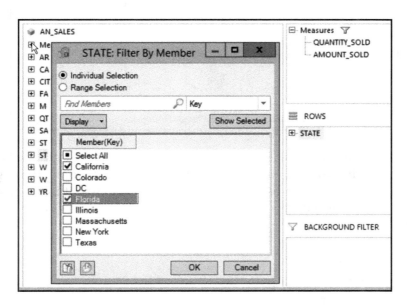

4. In the STATE | **Filter By Member** dialog box, deselect the **Select All** checkbox.

5. Select the California and Florida checkboxes and choose **OK**.

6. To display all again, right-click the STATE attribute in the **ROWS** panel and choose **Select All** members:

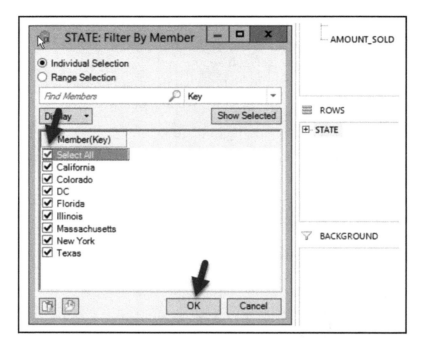

7. To display all except California, you can select the cell containing the word California and position your cursor on the edge of this cell so that the crosslines icon appears. Then, drag it to the blank cell area of the workbook to remove it.

7. In our AN_SALES view, we have a defined level hierarchy for the articles that are organized into categories and families. Therefore, we'll have to remove CATEGORY from **ROWS**. To do so, we follow these steps:

    1. Go to **DATA SOURCE** and then ARTICLE:

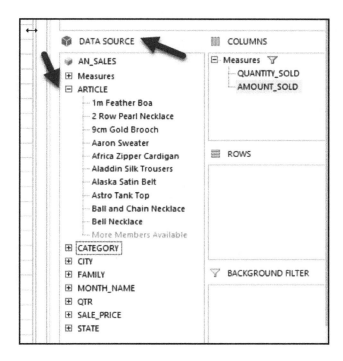

    2. In the **ROWS** panel, right-click STATE and choose **Remove**
    3. Drag HIER_FAM_CAT_ARTICLE to the **ROWS** pane
    4. In the workbook, expand the + icon under the ARTICLE column several times to navigate and expand the hierarchy

8. (Optional) you can also create a restricted measure on the fly from BusinessObjects Analysis. Let's see how can we do this:

   1. Choose the cell that's called, AMOUNT_SOLD.

   2. Choose **Calculations** ❘ **Add Restriction**:

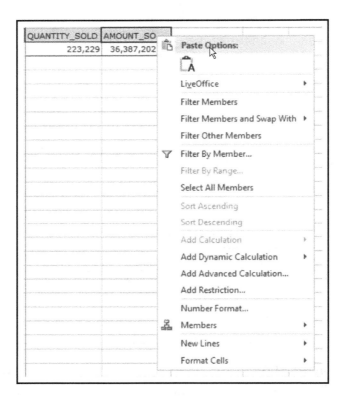

   3. Enter the name, Restricted Sales_YYYY (or a name that you want to enter).

   4. In the drop-down list, select AMOUNT_SOLD. In the selections box, use the drop-down list and choose the YR dimension:

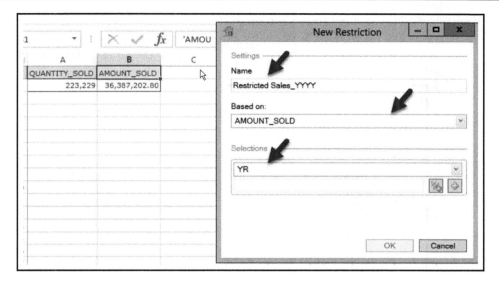

5. Choose **Open Value Help**, select the year **YYYY,** deselect all other checkboxes, and click **OK**:

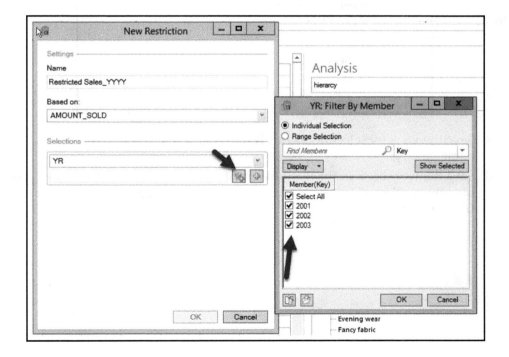

6. The new column is added and now we can add the measure into the **DATA SOURCE** panel by expanding the measure node and dragging the year `Restricted Sales_YYYY` into the **COLUMNS** panel:

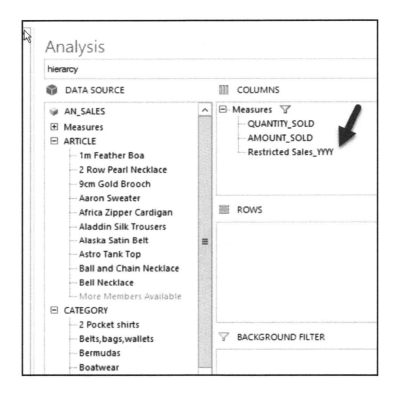

9. Save the view by selecting **Save View** and give it a name, `Analysis_view_HANA`.

10. Save the workbook in the BusinessObjects platform, choose **File** | **Analysis**, and save the workbook to a platform. Save the workbook to the SAP BusinessObjects BI platform:

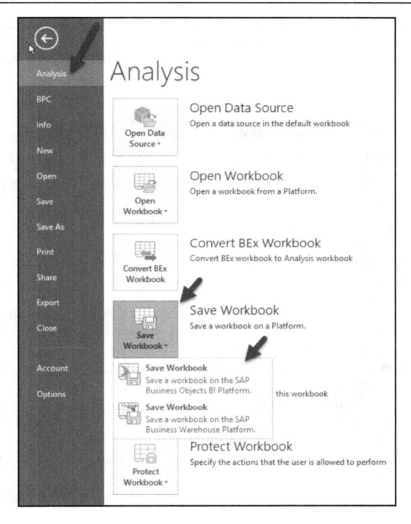

11. Reopen and refresh the workbook:
    1. Choose **File** | **Analysis.** Open the workbook from the platform
    2. Choose the `Analysis_view_HANA` view that we saved previously
    3. In **Analysis**, choose **Refresh All**

With these steps, we have created an SAP BusinessObjects Analysis workbook based on an existing SAP HANA calculation view. When you click on **Refresh All**, it'll update the corresponding data and redraw the crosstab with the newly created workbook based on the SAP HANA calculation view.

Creating a SAP BusinessObjects Analysis workbook based on an existing BEx query

Now, let's see how we can create a SAP BusinessObjects Analysis workbook based on an existing BEx query:

1. Start BusinessObjects Analysis, the Microsoft Excel edition, go to the options and then mark **Preferred Platform** as **Selectable**.
2. Like before, this will allow us to choose either NetWeaver or BI platform so that we can save our workbooks.
3. Insert the BEx query `U00_SAPB1_Q1` starting at cell **A1** (this query is available via the connection **BW_RWB_OLAP**, in the **Area** BW training. Go to **Customer Training** | **T_SAPBI** | eFashion cube. As we would be using the same template data, use query and Universe from `eFashion`).
4. The system will prompt for a username and password for BI platform; enter these details.
5. In the query, remove all the attributes from **ROWS,** and then add STATE, STORE, and CATEGORY, in this order. Then, swap the STATE and STORE columns directly in the body of the workbook. Change the order of Measures.
6. Restore the initial order of Measures and characteristics. Make sure that the report does not refresh after each action.
7. Remove the STORE attribute from **ROWS** and define the following filter settings for STATE:
    1. Display California and Florida
    2. Display all again
    3. Display all except California

8. The mock up data has an organization of categories called **category hierarchy one** related to gender. We can display this hierarchy in our workbook.

SAP BW has a special feature called **external hierarchies**. This feature is a rollup tree for any master data stored separately from the transactional dataset. These external relationships can be applied in any workbook that contains the base `InfoObject`.

9. Now we will just keep `CATEGORY` and `STATE` in **ROWS**, and sort the result set by `CATEGORY` (descending).

10. Filter the result set by the `AMOUNT_SOLD` measure to only include the top three amounts sold.

11. Remove the top N filter on `AMOUNT_SOLD` and add a custom local calculation percent contribution by `AMOUNT_SOLD`.

12. We can save `STATE` of our analysis as an analysis view called `BW_State_and_Category`.

13. Save our workbook in the BI platform and reopen and refresh the workbook we have just saved.

Report to report interface

Report to report interface allows us to link reports for drill-through reporting in SAP BW, with this you can call a jump target from a BEx query executed in Analysis. You can use the RRI to jump from the executed query (**Sender**) to another report (**Receiver**) containing more information. It allows the drilled down from **InfoCube** to **DSO** objects for more detailed reporting. You can call targets in BW systems and beyond.

We can use the **Report Report Interface** (**RRI**) to call targets that we have defined in your query. To be able to call the targets from executed queries, you must define the targets for the query with the sender/receiver assignment. The sender/receiver assignment is defined in transaction RSBBS in the BW system.

To make the RRI work, we will have to fulfill the requirements of the SAP note 1739153—*SAP BW Backend requirements for Analysis Office 1.3 or higher.*

Let's take a look at the steps, which are as follows:

1. Go to the RSBBS transaction code in the BW system:

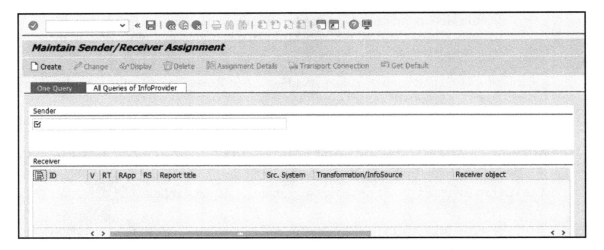

2. We need to select the query (this would be **Sender**) and then click on **Create**:

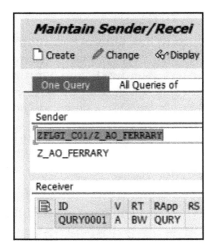

3. On the **Target System** area, we need to select the target system. We can choose to jump to the same system where we are working or another one:

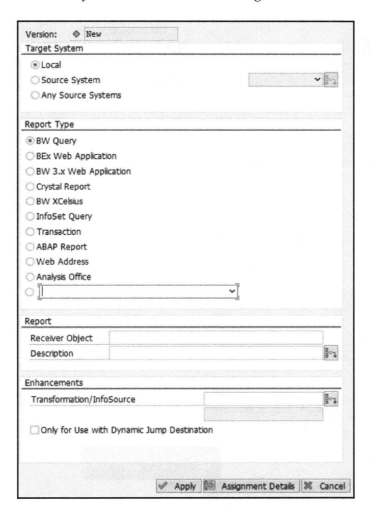

4. In the **Report** tab, choose the target query or object and click **Apply**. We will define the target for the report-to-report jump.

5. Now, when we open our sender query, we will be able to right click and select **Goto**:

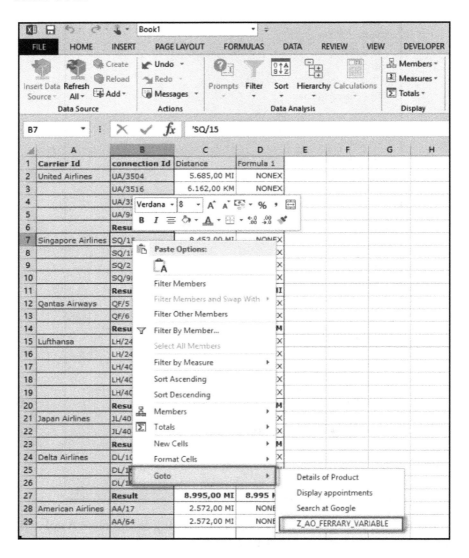

6. And we are able to jump to the target query:

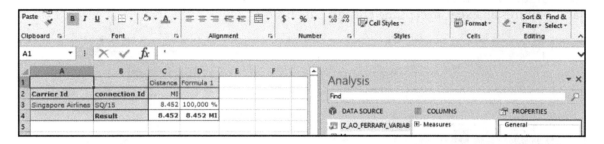

SAP BusinessObjects Analysis for Microsoft PowerPoint

In Microsoft PowerPoint, analysis is available as a separate tab in the ribbon. The ribbon is part of the Microsoft Office user interface, above the main work area that presents commands and options. Similar to Microsoft Excel, some Analysis options are available in the ribbon tab under **Start**.

Let's see how can we create a presentation using BusinessObjects Analysis for Microsoft PowerPoint. While, in Excel, the target users are analysts and business users, in PowerPoint, its target users are, to a further extent, business users. The use cases in PowerPoint also differ from Excel; in the latter, use cases are for the analysis and distribution of analysis (without building) while in PowerPoint, they're for the analysis and distribution of analysis (workbook building). The focus of Excel sheets is analysis and reporting while, in PowerPoint, the focus is more on reporting.

One comparison is that PowerPoint doesn't have all of the functionality of Excel but has some unique features of its own. The PowerPoint **Analysis** ribbon includes most of the same features as Excel, except the **Design** panel:

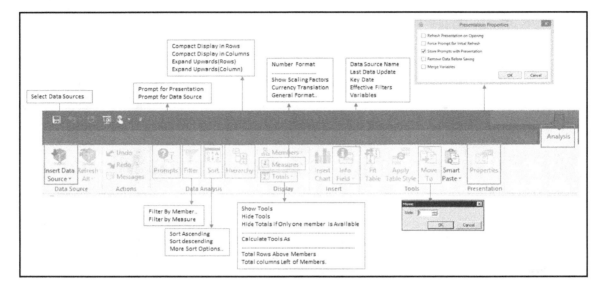

Overview of the PowerPoint Analysis ribbon

As shown in the preceding diagram, the **Analysis** tab contains the following groups, all of which are present under **File | Analysis**:

- **Data Source**
- **Actions**
- **Data Analysis**
- **Display**
- **Insert**
- **Tools**
- **Presentation**

Let's go through some of them in detail:

- **Data Source** has two options to choose from: **Insert Data Source** and **Refresh All**
- While with **Insert Data Source**, data from a source system can be inserted into a crosstab, **Refresh All** is used to refresh the data sources

Inserting a data source in a workbook

To analyze and create insights in the workbook, we need data. The sources for this data could be SAP BEx queries, query views, and SAP NetWeaver BW InfoProvider. The data is displayed in the workbook in crosstabs. We can insert multiple crosstabs in a workbook with data from different sources and systems. If the workbook is going to be used by different users, it is also helpful to add info fields with information on the data source and filter status. We can also plan business data based on the current data in our data source.

Let's walk through the process of inserting a data source into a workbook:

1. From the worksheet, choose the cell where the selected data source will be inserted.
2. Select **Insert Data Source** and log on to the SAP BusinessObjects BI platform dialogue box. Enter **User** and **Password**. Enter **WEB Service URL**.

 If you're logging on with the initial password (user of BW system), you might be asked to change your password.

3. Click on **OK**; this will take you to **Select Data Source**.
4. In the next screen, select **Show Connections**:
    1. By selecting **Select All**, **all present systems**, **Cubes/InfoProvider**, and **Query/Query view** are displayed on the BI platform
    2. If you tend to select **Query/Query view**, all present queries and query views are displayed on the BI platform
    3. If you make the selection of **Local System**, all systems in our local SAP log will be displayed
    4. By selecting **Cubes/InfoProvider**, all present cubes and InfoProvider will be displayed on the BI platform
    5. If you select **System**, all present systems will be displayed
5. After choosing the connection, click on **Next**:
    1. Based on the connection choice, you'll have different actions, for example, to select a query view or InfoProvider, you'll have to do a double-click to select the object.
    2. Then, select **Logon to System**.
    3. Enter your user log in details that you would have got from the administrator. Go to **Client**, enter **User** and **Password**, and then click on **OK**.

6. Now, we select **Data Source | OK**.
7. For the data sources based on SAP HANA, we can do the following:
   - **Search**: A wild card can be used before or after a partial string if we need to retrieve data sources that have a unique pattern. **Search** selection can be based on **description**, **technical name**, or **All**.
   - **Area**: We can choose either **All**, **Cube**, **Attribute**, or **Dimension View** and, based on what we choose, it'll display the objects.
8. Similarly, for the BW system, we can do the following:
   - **Search**
   - **Area**
   - **Workspace**
   - **Role**
9. Now, a new crosstab should be with us, consisting of the data from the selected data source that's inserted into the worksheet. Some of the groups are mentioned as follows; this will give you an overview of the uses of these groups:
   - **Data Analysis**: This group consists of mainly **Prompts**, **Filter**, **Sort**, and **Hierarchy**:
     - **Prompts**: This is used for query parameters and variable values
     - **Filter**: This is used to define the filtering criteria
     - **Sort**: This helps to quickly identify the data
     - **Hierarchy**: This is used to define hierarchy options such as parent child position and level
   - **Presentation**: In this group, we can specify settings for analysis in Microsoft PowerPoint:
     - **Refresh Presentation on Opening**: By selecting this, each time the presentation is opened, the data sources are refreshed. If this isn't selected, the data in the presentation isn't automatically refreshed on opening. It's also possible to do a manual refresh by choosing **Refresh All**.
     - **Force Prompt for Initial Refresh**: On every refresh, the prompting dialogue gets displayed.
     - **Store Prompt with Presentation**: The defined prompt values are saved with the presentation.

- **Remove Data Before Saving**: When this option is marked, the presentation will get saved without the data. When you reopen the presentation, the data won't be displayed. To have the data displayed, you'll have to choose **Refresh All**.

- **Insert**: The group contains the **Charts** and **Info Filed** tabs:
    - **Charts**: Used to insert dynamic charts. The chart is added according to the configuration. It's automatic when you change the displayed data in the crosstab.
    - **Info Field**: This is used for inserting information fields to provide additional information on data displayed in the workbook sheets.

Creating a PowerPoint presentation using SAP BusinessObjects Analysis for PowerPoint

Now, let's create a PowerPoint presentation using SAP BusinessObjects Analysis for PowerPoint based on the SAP HANA data and SAP BW data using an **Analysis** view.

Analysis for PowerPoint doesn't have the ability to add dimensions and, by default navigation, the SAP HANA view doesn't show any dimensions.

We'll start with the SAP HANA data as a source for PowerPoint:

1. Start **Analysis** for Microsoft PowerPoint:
    1. Go to Windows and then **All Programs**, choose **SAP Business Intelligence** and then **SAP BusinessObjects Analysis,** and select **Analysis for Microsoft PowerPoint**
    2. Click on **Blank Presentation** and open the **Analysis** tab
    3. Choose **Insert Data Source** and insert the **Analysis** view
2. Log on to the BI platform via SAP authentication using the following credentials and then insert the State_and_Category_BW view:
    1. Choose the Favorites folder and select the State_And_Category_HANA view
    2. If required, enter your SAP HANA user and password
    3. Choose **OK**

3. To understand the issues with presenting large amounts of data in PowerPoint, remove all but the first 12 rows of data:
    1. In the **Fit Table** dialog box, set the maximum number of rows to 12
    2. Check the **Abbreviate table** option on this slide
    3. Choose **OK**
4. Turn on scaling factors and sort the data in ascending order by doing the following:
    1. Click somewhere in the result set.
    2. In the **Analysis** ribbon, choose Measures.
    3. As you can see, scaling factors are already enabled. The currency is now displayed in each row.
    4. Choose **Sort | Ascending**.
5. Use the **Fit Table** option to split one slide into three:
    1. In the **Analysis** ribbon, choose **Fit Table**
    2. Select 4 for the number of rows
    3. Choose **split table** across multiple slides
    4. Choose **OK**
6. Add a chart to your presentation on a new slide:
    1. In the **Slides** tab on the left, right-click on the last slide and choose **New Slide**.
    2. Delete the PowerPoint textboxes for title and text.
    3. Navigate to the slide before the blank slide and click somewhere in the result set. Choose **Charts**, and a new chart will appear on the slide.
    4. With the chart selected, choose **Move To** and enter the slide number of the last slide.
    5. Choose **OK**. The chart will appear on the last slide.
7. Add **Key Date Info Field** to the first slide:
    1. Navigate to the first slide
    2. If necessary, resize the table to provide room at the top of the slide
    3. Click somewhere in the result set and choose **Info Filed | Key Date**
    4. Move the **Key Date** textbox so that it appears at the top of the slide

8. Save your analysis presentation with a name and description of `PowerPoint_HANA_Analysis` to the `Favorite` folder:
   1. Choose **File** | **Analysis** and save the presentation to the SAP BusinessObjects BI platform
   2. Choose the `Favorites` folder
   3. Enter the name and description shown previously
   4. Choose **Save**

Creating a PowerPoint presentation using analysis for PowerPoint based on SAP BW data

Now, we'll create a PowerPoint presentation using analysis for PowerPoint from the **Analysis** view from the SAP BW data. We'll use another view (not the same one as earlier in SAP HANA) just so it's not monotonous. Here, I'll use the **Product Plan and Actuals** view (from SAP BW); you can choose any BW view that's available in your system:

1. Start Analysis for Microsoft PowerPoint:
   1. Go to Windows, then **All Programs** | **SAP Business Intelligence** | **SAP BusinessObjects Analysis**, and then **Analysis for Microsoft PowerPoint**:

2. In **Blank Presentation**, open the **ANALYSIS** tab
3. Choose **Insert Data Source** and insert the **Analysis** view:

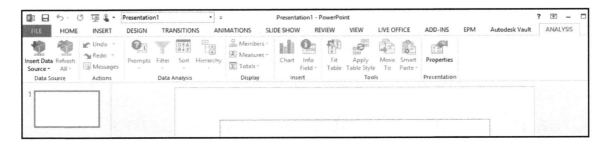

2. Log on to the BI platform via SAP authentication using the following credentials, and then insert the **Product Plan and Actuals** view. If required, enter your BW **User** and **Password**:

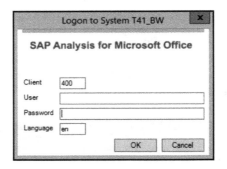

3. Go to the **Search** tab and select **Product Plan and Actuals**:

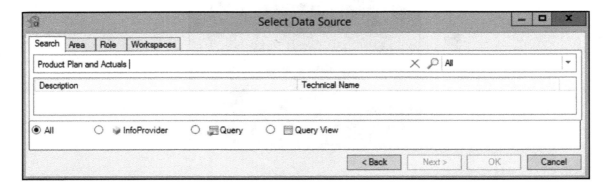

4. Choose **OK** and, selecting the view, you'll see the following screenshot:

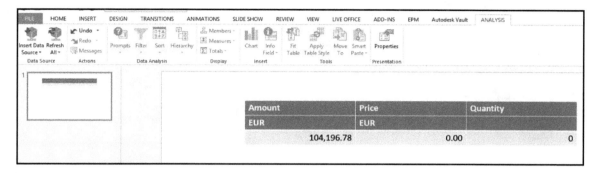

5. We need to turn the scaling factor and sort the data by ascending order:
   1. In the **Analysis** ribbon, select `Measures`
   2. Choose **Sort | Ascending**
   3. Choose **Fit Table | split table across multiple slides | OK**

6. Let's add a chart to our presentation on a new slide:
   1. Choose **New slide**.
   2. Delete the PowerPoint textboxes and text.
   3. Click somewhere in the result set and choose **Chart**. A new chart will appear on the slide:

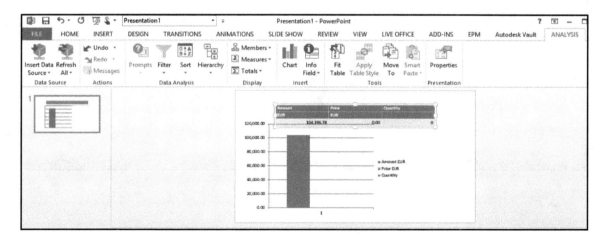

7. Choose **Move To**, enter the slide number of the last slide, and click on **OK**:

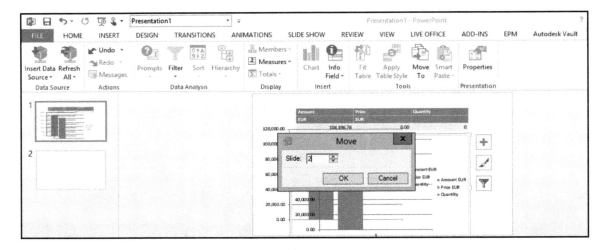

8. When you right-click on the chart, you will be given various options for that you can format it. You can choose them as needed:

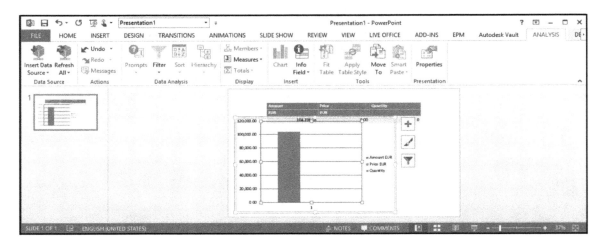

9. Add the key data **Info Field** to the first slide:
   1. Navigate to the first slide and resize the table at the top of the slide
   2. Click somewhere and choose **Info Field | Key Date**:

10. Save the presentation:
    1. Go to **FILE | ANALYSIS** and save presentation to the SAP BusinessObjects BI platform
    2. Enter the **Name** and **Description**
    3. Click on **Save**

Through these steps, we have created a PowerPoint presentation using analysis for PowerPoint using both the SAP HANA data and SAP BW data.

Summary

With this chapter, we became familiar with SAP BusinessObjects Analysis for Microsoft. We learned how to create a basic workbook with SAP BusinessObjects Analysis for Microsoft and created a presentation using BusinessObjects Analysis for Microsoft PowerPoint. We discussed the features and capabilities of SAP BusinessObjects Analysis for Microsoft Office in detail and took a deep look at data connectivity in SAP BusinessObjects Analysis for Microsoft Office. With the know-how of SAP BusinessObjects Analysis for Microsoft, you can (irrespective of whether you're a business analyst or business user) easily do some of core tasks, all without any help from the IT department.

In the next chapter, we'll learn about SAP BusinessObjects Design Studio, where we'll walk through various concepts related to Design Studio, namely initial view, layout, and architecture. We'll end the chapter with a use case where we'll create an analytical application with a **Tabstrip** layout and **Filter** panels.

3
SAP BusinessObject Design Studio

SAP BusinessObjects Design Studio is a tool that's used to create analysis applications and dashboards for web browsers and handheld devices with the help of SAP BW and SAP HANA data sources. In this chapter, we will learn about SAP BusinessObjects Design Studio and discuss a variety of its features, including the initial view, layout, and architecture. We will end this chapter by creating an analytical application with a **Tabstrip** layout and filter panels.

In this chapter, we will cover the following topics:

- SAP BusinessObjects Design Studio
- Initial view and layout
- Design Studio architecture
- Creating an analytical application

Before we begin, it's important to know that since Q3 2017, we do not have a separate product offering for SAP BusinessObjects Design Studio. Instead, SAP has SAP BusinessObjects Lumira 2.0 as its next major version for both SAP Lumira 1.x and SAP BusinessObjects Design Studio 1.x. This means that as of now, we have the following diagram:

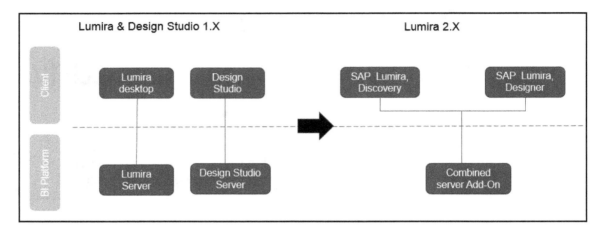

 This chapter is intended to serve all those readers who have Design Studio 1.x in their landscape and would like to learn about it. For those of you who are already on Lumira 2.x, you should skip this chapter.

Introduction to SAP BusinessObjects Design Studio

SAP's BI client portfolio is very wide and offers multiple tools. SAP BusinessObjects Design Studio is for those users who want to consume models from SAP HANA and SAP BW. In the following diagram, we can clearly see the various tools from the **Common Platform Service** and **Interoperability**:

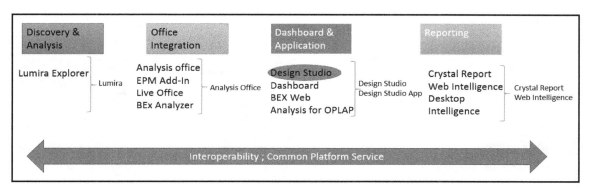

Some of the salient features of SAP BusinessObjects Design Studio are as follows:

- It facilitates pre-built templates with guided procedures for faster design
- It can consume **Key Performance Indicators** (**KPIs**) directly from SAP HANA, semantic layers, and SAP BW
- It has a flexible SDK to customize visualizations, dashboards, and apps
- It facilitates the reusability of queries, InfoCubes, SAP HANA, and other data models/marts
- It has an Eclipse-based design environment that is easy to scale

From a usage perspective, an IT and business team might use the same/different Design Studio technologies, depending on their needs and scenario. In the following diagram, we can classify and see the interaction between various Design Studio technologies and how IT and businesses can use them:

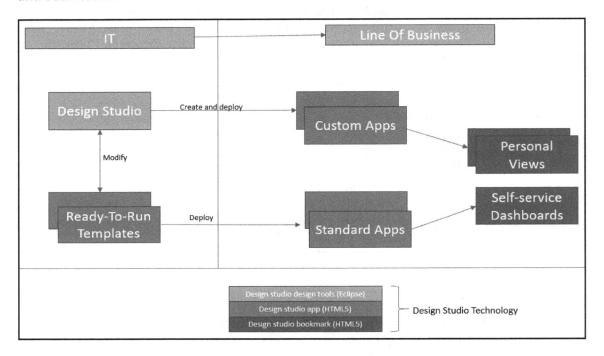

Interface elements of SAP BusinessObjects Design Studio

SAP BusinessObjects Design Studio enables you to analyze and visualize data. You can do any of the following:

- Visualize data from multiple sources and combine them into one story
- Create different visualizations for story composition
- Visualize data with BW hierarchies
- Filter data on the basis of dimensions
- Use pivot tables and standard context menus

To support all of the preceding features and capabilities, SAP BusinessObjects Design Studio has the following interface elements:

- **Menu**
- **Filter Area**
- **Navigation Area**
- **Setting Area for Chart and Table**
- **Data Area**
- **Action Area**
- **Data Connection**
- **Chart Type Picker**
- **Navigation Panel**
- **Filter Line**
- **Bookmark Functionality**
- **Context Menu**

Working with the design tool

The design tool consists of the **Components**, **Outline**, and **Properties** views, as well as the layout editor, menu, and toolbar. We will learn about some of these in this section.

The **Components** view contains all of the components that can be used for creating analysis applications. These components are part of the user interface, and their behavior can be edited in the **Properties** view. Based on their functions, they are group into different folders:

- **Analytic Components** are used to visualize data. This group contains the following components:
  - **Chart**
  - **Crosstab**

In the following screenshot, you can see the **Analytic Components** listed:

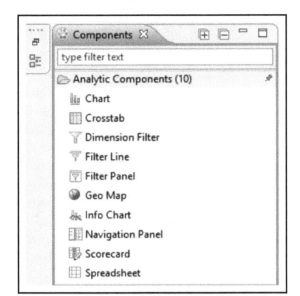

With **Crosstab**, you can display multi-dimensional data in a table with analytical functions.

- **Basic Components** is a set of multiple components with different functions that can be used at design time (**Button**, **Image**, and **Text**) or at runtime (**Dropdown Box**). For example, components such as **Dropdown Box** and **Checkbox** are meant for select and filter, while components such as **Text** and **data field** are for layout and design. This group contains the following components:
  - **Dropdown Box**
  - **Button**
  - **Checkbox**
  - **Date Field**
  - **Image**
  - **Input filed**
  - **List box**
  - **Radio button**
  - **Text**

You can see some of the **Basic Components** listed in the following screenshot:

- **Container Components** are used to group and structure the content of an application. They also help to optimize applications for mobile devices. This group contains the following components:
    - **Grid Layout**
    - **Pagebook**
    - **Panel**
    - **Popup**
    - **Split Cell Container**
    - **Tabstrip**

The following screenshot shows the list of **Container Components**:

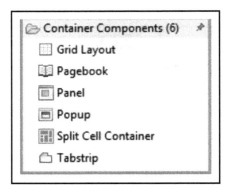

- The **Outline** view contains all the data sources and UI components. With this view, we can get a hierarchical overview of any application that is opened in the editor. Drag and drop works for the **Outline** view as well:
    - We can easily assign charts to data sources with the help of drag and drop components (like **Crosstab**).
    - By moving/dragging and dropping components within the **Outline** view (within the same container to change the order of UI components, or between different containers).
    - By dragging and dropping components from the **Components** view onto another container UI element in the **Outline** view. The following screenshot shows a hierarchical overview of an application that has been opened in the editor:

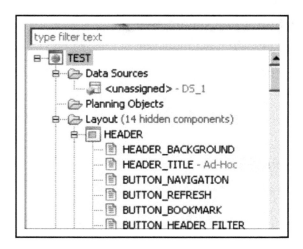

- The **Properties** view is used to view the properties of a selected object (which is currently open). You can select multiple components. This selection is only possible for the **Outline** view (where a **Property** sheet is displayed). The properties that are common to all selected components are displayed and can be edited as well (simultaneously). In the following screenshot, you can see the **Properties** view:

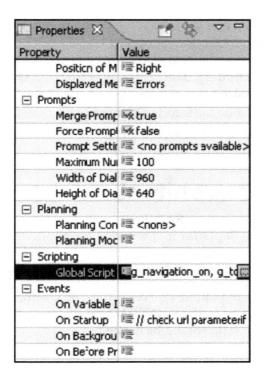

The multi-editing function is only possible for simple properties.

- The **Layout** editor provides users with the capability to edit applications in the editor area. It has a **Standard Widget Toolkit** (**SWT**) browser control. Depending on the operating system, it can be embedded in a browser, or a browser can be embedded in a SWT browser. For example, **Microsoft Edge** is embedded in a SWT browser in the Windows operating system, while in other operating systems, browsers such as Mozilla and Safari are embedded. In the **Layout** editor, you can do the following:
  - Drag and drop from the **Components** view to the editor area, thus creating a new component
  - Assign the data source to the target components by dragging and dropping a data source alias from the **Outline** view onto a **Data Binding** component
  - Update the selected components in the **Outline** view
  - Update the **Outline** and **Properties** views

Design Studio architecture

Depending on the need and use case, SAP BusinessObjects Design Studio can be used both locally and integrated in the BI platform. If we need the application just for evaluation/prototype purposes, we can create it in local mode. However, for a productive solution, we have to switch to the BI platform by adding data sources.

The prerequisite for using a BI platform server is that the **Online Analytical Processing** (**OLAP**) data source connection to the SAP HANA system or to the **SAP NetWeaver BW** systems containing business data should be created.

Let's take a deeper look at the various deployment options.

Deployment platform as BI

The following are some of the key points related to this deployment:

- Available since Design Studio 1.0
- The Design Studio applications are stored on a BI platform
- It has the ability to connect to multiple SAP BW and SAP HANA systems via the **Central Management Console** (**CMC**)

- Promotion management is used to transport the applications from development to production
- It is a prerequisite for SAP BI mobile solutions

The following is an architecture for the deployment of Design Studio on the SAP BusinessObjects BI platform:

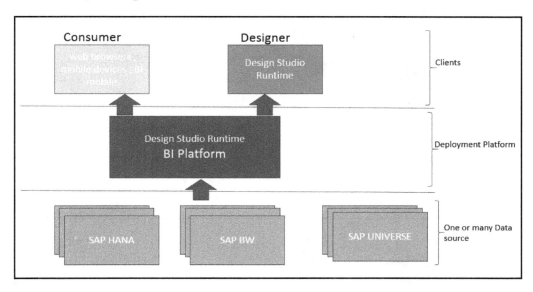

Deployment on SAP NetWeaver

The following are some of the key points related the deployment of SAP NetWeaver. The limitation of this deployment is that it can only be connected to one BW system:

- Available since Design Studio 1.0
- The Design Studio applications are stored on SAP BW
- Can only connect to one BW system
- Transport is done via the ABAP transport concept; therefore it is done through different systems using transaction log objects
- Applications developed on this deployment are portable on devices

This following is an architecture for the deployment of Design Studio on NetWeaver:

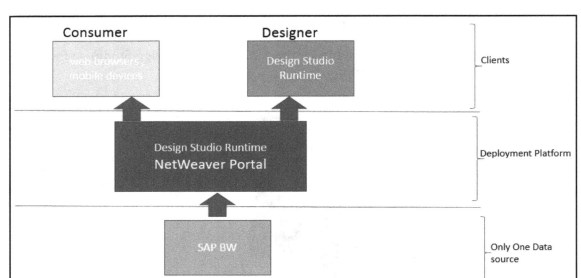

In cases where a connection is with a SAP NetWeaver BW or SAP HANA system, we can also work with inactive connections when designing and validating the data sources for this connection. The connection is automatically active when the backend system (SAP HANA or SAP NetWeaver BW) is up and running.

Deployment on SAP HANA

The following are some of the key points related to this deployment option:

- Available since Design Studio 1.3
- The Design Studio applications are stored on a SAP HANA repository
- Direct native connectivity to HANA's **Info Access Service (InA)** via Firefly

The following is an architecture for the deployment of Design Studio on SAP HANA:

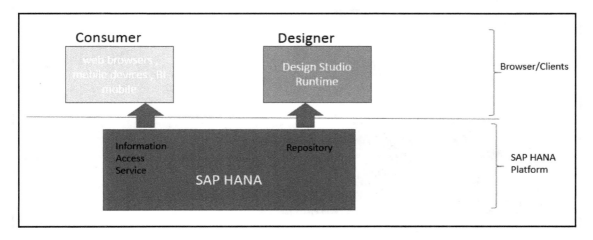

Architecture for local mode

This mode is only used for prototyping. The default setting (post installation) for SAP BusinessObjects Design Studio is local mode, which can be used to create analysis applications for presentation and evaluation purposes, as this would be on the local system of the user.

The following are some of the key points related to this deployment option:

- Only used for quick demos and prototypes
- Direct connection to backend data sources by using the local SAP `logon.ini` file and ODBC HANA connection information
- Design Studio Java applications run locally on a laptop or system

The following is an architecture for the local deployment of Design Studio:

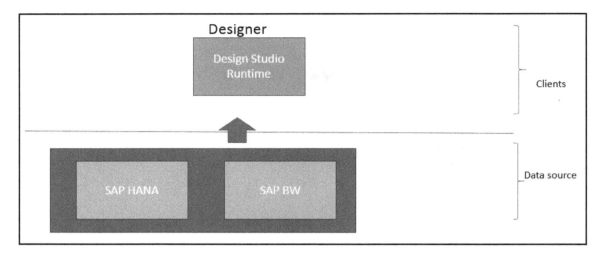

In the BI platform, we can easily switch from the default startup mode in the **Preferences** dialog box and connect to the BI platform. Then, we can upload our locally saved analysis applications to the BI platform.

Use case – creating an analytical application

To create an analytical application, we can use any of the three different data sources, which are SAP HANA view, SAP BO Universe, and BW query. In our use case, we will use SAP HANA view as the data source, and then look at the process of using SAP BO Universe. You can try creating (on your own) an analytical application with BW query, as the steps are very similar to what we will see with SAP HANA and SAP BO Universe.

Let's get started and create an application in SAP BusinessObjects Design Studio, using SAP HANA view as the data source. Here, we will again reuse the same HANA views that we had from `eFashion` (`CALC_AN_SALES`). Perform the following steps:

1. First, we need to make sure that **Preferred Startup Mode** for Design Studio is SAP BusinessObjects BI platform. If it isn't, then we need to change it and then restart Design Studio.

> To change startup mode, go to **Tools** | **Preferences** in **Application Design** | **Preferred Startup Mode** | **SAP Business Object BI platform**. Then, you need to restart Design Studio. In our case, we used SAP HANA as the source and then SAP BO Universe. This means that we can toggle between them.

2. Let's change this to SAP HANA. Go to **Tools** | **Preferences**, like so:

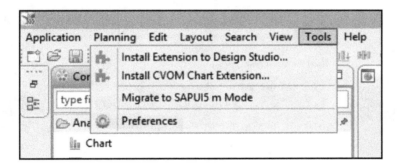

3. Then, in **Application Design** | **Preferred Startup Mode**, choose **SAP HANA** from the drop-down, as follows:

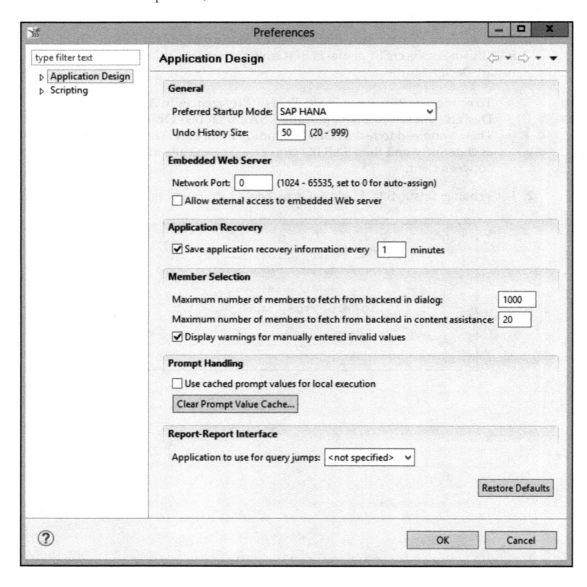

4. Log on to the SAP BusinessObjects BI platform and select **Create Analysis Application**:

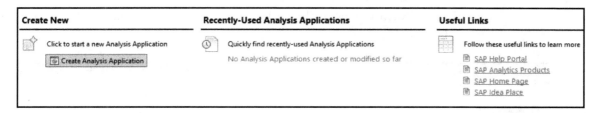

5. Enter the name of the application (for example, DS_App01) and select **Standard | Blank | Create**:

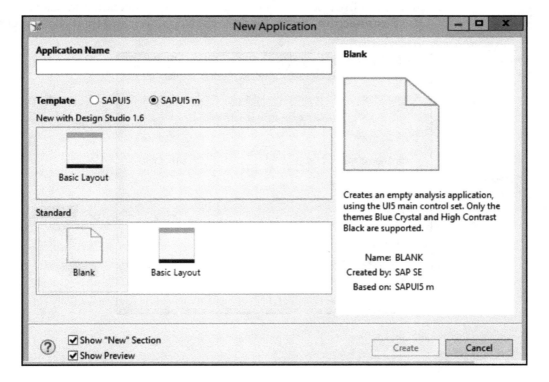

6. Make sure that the view is accessible via **OLAP connection**.

7. Create a data source (DS_1) based on the calculation view, CALC_AN_SALES:

1. We should first make sure that **OLAP connection** is in place and that it's working (check with your SAP BO administrator for this).

2. In the **Outline** pane, right-click on **Data Source** and select **Add Data Source**:

3. Choose the **Browse** button in your selected connection and select **OLAP connection** (this is for SAP HANA view), and then click on **OK**:

4. Choose the **Browse** button that's located next to the **Data Source** field to expand the eFashion folder and select CALC_AN_SALES. Then, click on **OK**:

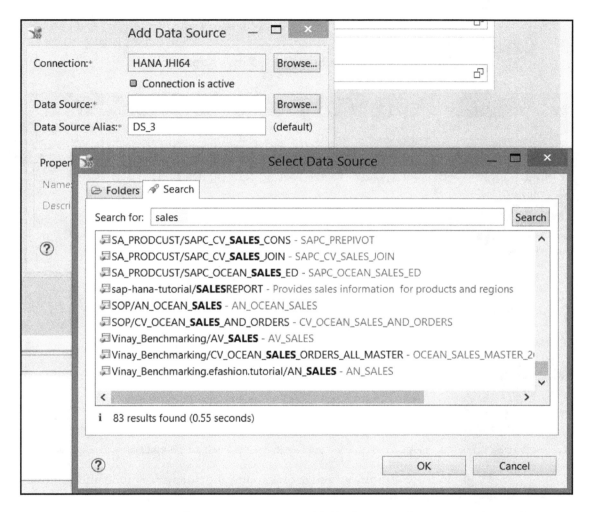

5. The data source (DS_1) is added (the preceding screenshot is for DS_3 as we will be using it later; the process, however, remains the same).

8. Display the sales amount for each store on a chart:
   1. Before we can proceed any further, we have to check that the initial view on the data source (DS_1) has the STORE attribute in **Rows** and the AMOUNT_SOLD measure in **Columns**.
   2. Right-click on CALC_AN_SALES (in the eFashion folder) and choose **Edit Initial View**.
   3. Drag the STORE attribute to the **Rows** screen area:

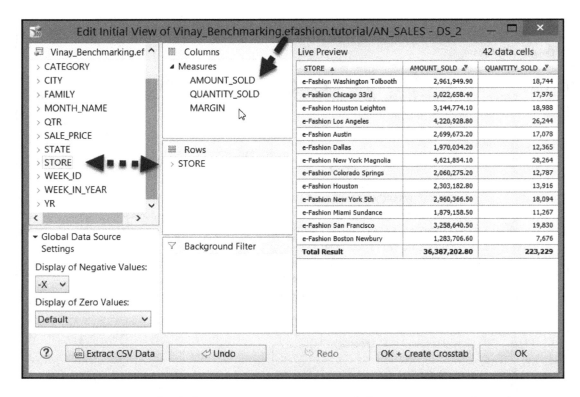

   4. In the **Columns** screen area, expand the Measures node and remove all measures except AMOUNT_SOLD by right-clicking on the Measures node and selecting **Remove** I **OK**.
   5. In the **Analytic Components** screen area, drag the **Chart** component onto the canvas and select the chart.
   6. In the **Properties** view pane, go to **Data Binding** I DS_1 under **Display**, and select **Crosstab** from the **Chart Type** drop-down list.

9. Now, we will create a line chart that shows the amount sold measure for each calendar year:
    1. We will create a copy of `DS_1` and edit its initial view so that it shows the data that we need for the chart. Right-click on `eFashion | CALC_AN_SALES_DS1`, copy it, and then right-click again to paste it.
    2. A new data source will be created—`eFashion | CALC_AN_SALES_DS2`.
    3. Now, we will edit the initial view of this newly created data source. Right-click on the data source (`eFashion | CALC_AN_SALES_DS2`) and select **Edit Initial View**.
    4. In the **Rows** screen area, remove `STORE` and add `YR`. Click **OK**.
    5. In the **Analytic Components** screen area, drag the **Chart** component onto the canvas and select the chart.
    6. In the **Properties** pane, under **Data Binding**, choose `DS2` from the drop-down list under **Display** and select **Line** from the **Chart Type** drop-down list.
    7. Under **Display**, select **True** from the **Swap Axes** drop-down list.
10. As the next step, we need to create a table showing the `AMOUNT_SOLD` measure for the characteristics state, store, and year:
    1. Again, we create a copy of the data source `DS_1` with the alias `DS_3`. Data source `DS_3` is created.
    2. Right-click `eFashion | CALC_AN_SALES–DS3` and choose **Edit Initial View**:

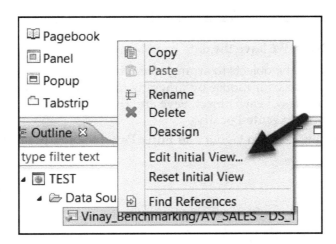

3. Drag and drop elements until the **Rows** screen area contains STATE, STORE, AMOUNT_SOLD and QUANTITY_SOLD. Then, choose **OK + Create Crosstab**:

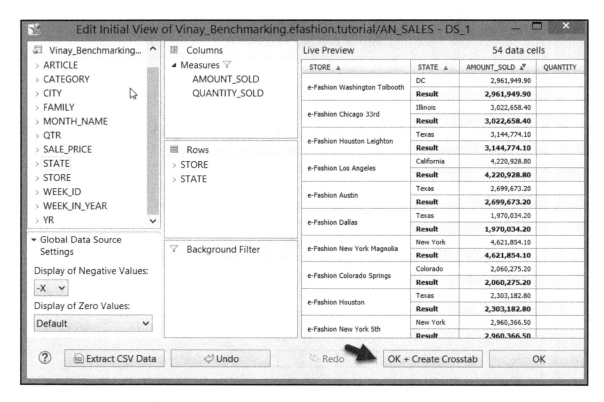

4. Now, we have the data and objects that we need for the chart.

11. Drag and drop the objects to arrange them into the order you desire. You can resize them with your mouse by dragging the resize handles located on the corners and sides of each object. Save and then click on **Execute Locally** (**Application | Execute Locally**).

12. Now, add the **Tabstrip** layout and **Filter Panel** to our application.

13. In the **Outline** pane, right-click on the `Layout` folder and choose **Create Child | Tabstrip** (this is the same as dragging it onto the canvas from the **Components** pane):

    1. In the **Layout** section, select the `TABSTRIP_1` component:

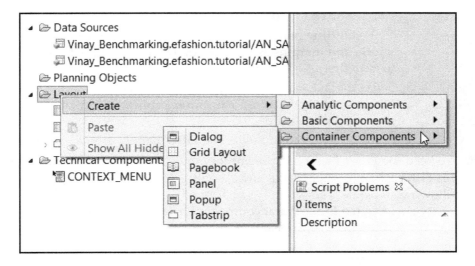

    2. In the **Properties** pane, change the attribute values for the margins, width, and height (set the width and height to auto first).
    3. In the **Outline** pane, right-click the new component, `TABSTRIP_1`, and choose the **Create Child** tab.
    4. In the **Layout** section (of the **Outline** pane), choose `TAB_1`.
    5. In the **Display** section (of the **Properties** pane), change the attribute from **Text to Pie.**
    6. Similarly, rename the `TAB_2` tab to **line** and `TAB_3` to `crosstab`:

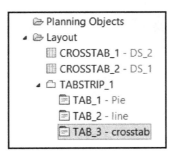

14. Adjust and resize the components relative to the tab so that they have the same height, width, and margins as **Tabstrip** that we created in a previous step. We set the system to default and open the application on TAB_3 (**crosstab**) when opened:

    1. In the **Outline** pane, drag CHART_1 to TAB_1, CHART_2 to TAB_2, and CROSSTAB_1 to TAB_3.

    2. In the **Outline** pane, select each chart and **Crosstab** and set the height, width, and margins as you did for **Tabstrip** (set the height and width to auto first).

    3. Select the TABSTRIP_1 component. In the **Properties** pane, under **Display**, set the **Selected Tab Index** property to **2** (zero is the first tab, so second is the third).

    4. Now, we are ready to place the **Filter Panel**.

15. We need the **Filter Panel** component for the DS_3 data source to the canvas. Set this **Filter Panel** to filter STATE and YR only. This can be done by performing the following steps:

    1. Drag the **Filter Panel** component from the **Analytic Components** pane to the right of **Crosstab** in TAB_3:

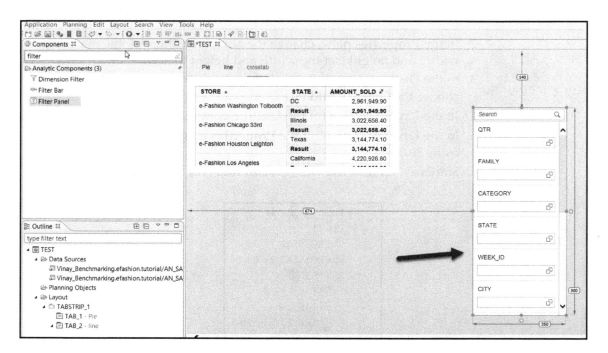

2. Drag the DS_3 data source onto the FILTERPANEL_1 component.

3. In the **Outline** pane, select the FILTERPANEL_1 component.

4. In the **Properties** pane, select the **Display Dimensions** property and choose the **Edit Dimensions** list button.

5. Remove all the dimensions, except STATE and YR, and click **OK**:

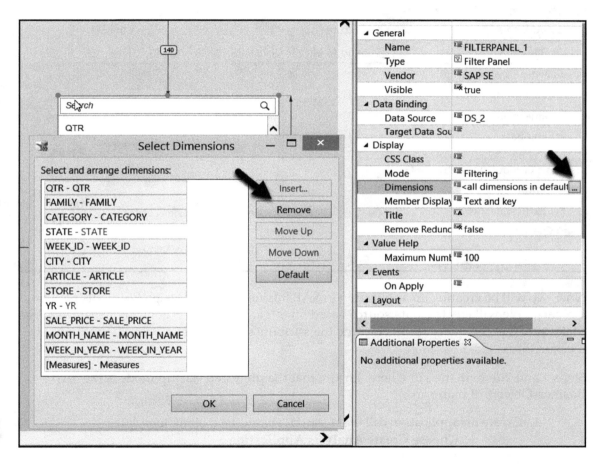

6. The complete application is ready to run locally.

16. Save and run the application:
    1. Save the application and name it APP02_DS.
    2. Choose **Application** and select **Execute Locally**:

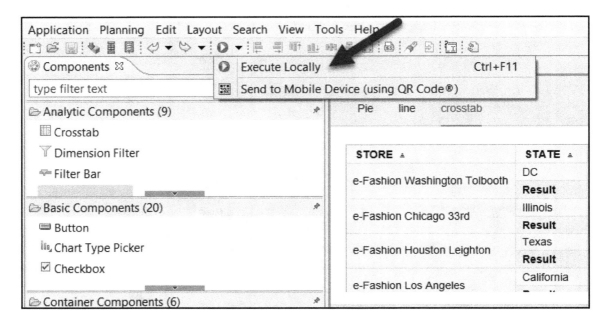

Now, we will be creating an application in SAP BusinessObjects Design Studio using SAP Universe. We will create a data source based on eFashiob.unx (WebI Universes) Universe. Make sure that the query results include the attribute's Store name, State, Year, and the measure of Sales revenue.

Steps 1 and 2 remain the same here. Ensure that the preferred startup mode is the SAP BusinessObjects BI platform:

1. Create an application called DS_App01, based on a blank template:
    1. Choose **Create Analysis Application**
    2. Name it DS_App01
    3. Select **Standard** | **Blank** | **Create**

2. Create a data source based on eFashion.unx. In the **Outline** view pane, right-click **Data Source** | **Add Data Source**:

   1. Choose the **Browser** | **Connection** field
   2. Select connection and choose eFashion.unx | **OK**
   3. Choose **Edit Query Specification**
   4. In the **Navigation** pane, expand the Store folder and drag the Store name to the results objects for the query pane
   5. Repeat the previous step for State
   6. In the **Navigation** pane, expand Time Period and drag Year to the results objects for the query pane
   7. Expand the Measures folder and drag Sales revenue to the results objects for the query pane
   8. Confirm **OK** (confirm the query specification)
   9. Confirm **OK** (to confirm that you have added the data source)

3. Create a pie chart to show the sale revenue:

   1. Make sure that the initial view on data source DS_1 has the Store name attribute in **Rows** and the Sales revenue measure in **Columns**.
   2. In the **Outline** view, right-click eFashion.unx-DS_1 and select **Edit Initial View**.
   3. Drag Store name to the **Rows** and choose **OK**.
   4. In **Analytic Components,** drag the **Chart** component onto the canvas and select the chart.
   5. Then, go to the **Properties** view pane and select **Data Binding**. Choose DS_1.
   6. Under **D**isplay, select **Pie** from **Chart Type**.

4. Now, we will create a table showing the Sales revenue measure for the characteristics State, Store name, and Year:

   1. Create a copy of DS_1 with the alias as DS_3, and edit the initial view setting
   2. Drag and drop elements until the **Rows** screen area contains State, Store name, and Year
   3. Choose **OK** and create **Crosstab**

5. Drag and drop to arrange the objects as you want them to be. Resize them with your mouse by dragging the resize handles located on the corners and sides of each object. Save these settings. Then, click on **Execute Locally** (**Application** | **Execute Locally**).

6. Now, we need to add the **Tabstrip** layout and **Filter Panel** to our application:

   1. In the **Outline** pane, right-click the `Layout` folder. Choose **Create Child | Tabstrip** (this is the same as dragging it onto the canvas from the **Components** pane).
   2. In the **Layout** section, select the `TABSTRIP_1` component.
   3. In the **Properties** pane, change the attribute values for the margins, width, and height (set the width and height to auto first).
   4. In the **Outline** pane, right-click on the new component, `TABSTRIP_1`, and choose **Create Child** tab.
   5. In the **Layout** section (of the **Outline** pane), choose `TAB_1`.
   6. In the **Display** section (of the **Properties** pane), change the attribute from **Text to Pie**.
   7. Similarly, rename `TAB_2` tab to **line** and the new tab to **crosstab**.

7. Adjust and resize the components relative to the tab so that they have the same height, width, and margins as the **Tabstrip** we created in a previous step. We set the system to default and opened the application on `TAB_3` (**crosstab**) when it was opened first:

   1. In the **Outline** pane, drag `CHART_1` to `TAB_1`, `CHART_2` to `TAB_2`, and `CROSSTAB_1` to `TAB_3`
   2. In the **Outline** pane, select each chart and **Crosstab** and set the height, width, and margins as you did for **Tabstrip** (set the height and width to auto first)
   3. Select the `TABSTRIP_1` component in **Properties** pane under **Display** and set the **Selected Tab Index** property to **2** (zero is the first tab, so two is the third)
   4. Now we are ready to place **Filter Panel**

8. Now, we will set the **Filter Panel** component for `DS_3` to the canvas. Set this **Filter Panel** to filter `STATE` and `YR` only. This can be done by following these steps:

   1. Drag the **Filter Panel** component from the **Analytic Components** pane to the right of **Crosstab** in `TAB_3`
   2. Drag the `DS_3` data source onto the `FILTERPANEL_1` component
   3. In the **Outline** pane, select the `FILTERPANEL_1` component
   4. In the **Properties** pane, select the **Display Dimensions** property and choose the **Edit Dimensions** list button
   5. Remove all the dimensions, except `STATE` and `YR`, and choose **OK**
   6. The complete application is ready to run locally

9. Save and run the application:
    1. Save the application and name it `APP03_DS`.
    2. Choose **Application** | **Execute Locally.**

Now, we are able to create an analytical application with the help of SAP Universe as well. In the previous two exercises, we showed you how we can create an analytical application using SAP Universe and SAP HANA view. Similarly, an analytical application using a BW query can also be created. I leave this to the readers as an exercise.

Summary

In this chapter, we became familiar with SAP BusinessObjects Design Studio. We learned about an analytical application in SAP BusinessObjects Design Studio by using various data sources (such as SAP HANA view and SAP Universe). We started this chapter with a general introduction to SAP BusinessObjects Design Studio and its features and capabilities. Then, we went deeper into its architectural aspect and deployment mode. Finally, we walked through each step of how to create an analytical application.

In the next chapter, we will learn about SAP BusinessObjects WebI. We will learn how to create an SAP BusinessObjects WebI document. We will learn how to query, report, and analyze with SAP BusinessObjects WebI. We will also walk through the concepts of breaks, WebI calculation, groups, and the data manager in WebI.

4

SAP BusinessObject Web Intelligence

In this chapter, you'll be introduced to the SAP BusinessObjects **Web Intelligence** (**WebI**) tool—what it is and the architectural concept for it. We will learn how to create a SAP BusinessObjects WebI document and how to use features like query, report, and analyze with SAP BusinessObjects WebI. We will also walk through the concepts of breaks, WebI calculation, groups, and the data manager in WebI. We will, just like in previous chapters, take `eFashion` as our source and create a WebI report step-by-step. This chapter should enable you to use SAP BusinessObjects WebI to view, analyze, and create reports based on data (for example sales, products, and stores) and get familiar with the basic functions of SAP BusinessObjects WebI.

In this chapter, we will cover the following topics:

- SAP BusinessObjects WebI
- Creating a WebI document
- Querying with SAP BusinessObjects WebI
- Reporting with SAP BusinessObjects WebI
- Analyzing with SAP BusinessObjects WebI

Introduction to SAP BusinessObjects WebI

WebI allows business users to dynamically create relevant data queries. By using this, you can apply filters to data which allows you to slice and dice, drill down, find exceptions, and create calculations in the data. It is very intuitive and helpful for ad hoc reporting and analysis.

Like most SAP applications, WebI uses a three-tier client-server architecture in which the functional process logic, data access, computer data storage, and user interface are developed and maintained as independent modules on separate platforms. It allows for different development teams to work on their own areas of expertise.

We are able to scale the application up and out. It gives us the ability to update the technology stack of one-tier, without impacting other areas of the application. The layers in WebI are:

- **Database layer**: This is the layer for the data source, which could be SAP or non-SAP
- **Semantic layer**: In this layer where the data models are created, which are later consumed/queried from the presentation layer
- **Presentation layer**: This is the user interface where data (in the desired report/dashboard) is presented to the user

These three layers can be represented as follows (in blue boxes):

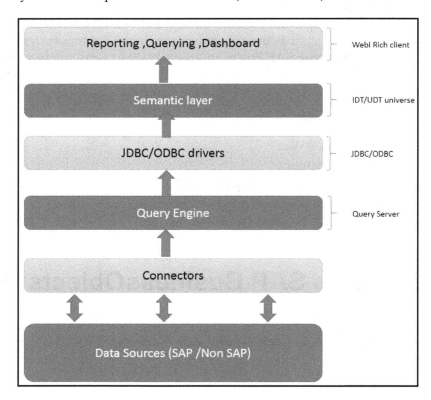

The BusinessObjects Enterprise technical architecture is composed of a set of tiers optimized for specific tasks and operations. While it has three-tier architecture as mentioned previously, it has connectors (to provide the connection between **Data Sources** and **Query Engine**) and Oracle database connection drivers (to all **Semantic layer** access the query results from **Query Server**). The **Semantic layer** is exposed to **Web Rich client** for **Reporting** and **Querying** via **Dashboard**.

With the ad hoc interactive reporting capability of SAP BusinessObjects WebI, you can do the following:

- Share, analyze, format, and access business insights (all in one tool)
- Create queries easily on your own (without a report designer)
- Query on any type of data source (with built-in features for analysis)

Let's discuss into some of its capabilities in detail.

Reporting with SAP BusinessObjects WebI

The document features of WebI allow you to create professional reports from the data that's retrieved. This data can be presented in various forms:

- As charts, such as bar charts, line charts, and pie charts
- As tables, such as crosstab tables, horizontal tables, vertical tables, and forms tables
- As multi-block reports containing huge volumes of data

Querying with SAP BusinessObjects WebI

With the help of the SAP BusinessObjects WebI query panel, we can add and organize objects and build queries. The following screenshot shows the query panel in action:

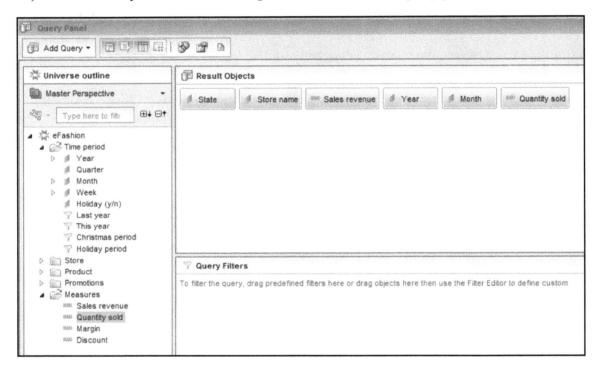

To build a query in the SAP BusinessObjects WebI query panel, we must select the Universe objects and **Query Filters** that represent our business question. In our example, we are connecting to the SAP BusinessObjects BI platform, so the query would be sent to the SAP BusinessObjects WebI server, which generates the final query statements. The query is then sent to the database to retrieve the data that was mapped to the objects we selected. The database returns this data to the SAP BusinessObjects WebI server, which populates the data as a data provider. This information is then formatted and displayed in a SAP BusinessObjects WebI document as a simple table, or even a complex chart, ready for our analysis.

Analyzing with SAP BusinessObjects WebI

SAP BusinessObjects WebI also allows you to analyze your reports and form your business perspective by moving objects, inserting calculations, and changing the display. These features allow you to decipher important information easily. You can also perform multidimensional analysis by looking at the results at a global level or exploring the information in detail by using the drill down option.

WebI calculations

SAP BusinessObjects WebI provides standard calculation functions that help you make faster calculations. This means that we do not need to write a logic or additional program but just call these functions. SAP BusinessObjects WebI has the following calculation functions as standard (different tool have different out of box functions available, so let's have a quick look at what is available with WebI and how it can be used):

- **Sum**: This function allows a user to calculate the sum of data (selected).
- **Count**: This calculation function helps us count all of the rows for a measured object or count distinct rows for a dimension or detailed project.
- **Minimum**: This function is used to display the minimum value of the selected data.
- **Average**: This function allows a user to calculate the average of the data.
- **Maximum**: In contrast to the minimum function, the maximum function is used to display the maximum value of the selected data.
- **Percentage**: This function displays the selected data as a percentage of the total (of selected data). The results of the percentage are displayed in an additional column or row of the table.
- **Default:** This function applies the default aggregation function to a standard measure, or the database aggregation function to a smart measure.

You can also use the formulas to build custom calculations. A **custom calculation** is a formula that can consist of report objects, functions, and operators.

Groups and sorts

Groups allow you to split the report into smaller and more comprehensible parts. For example, we can group quarterly revenue results into sections on a report. The grouped value appears as a header outside the block instead of remaining within the block when we are using breaks.

Please be remember that a section impacts the whole report page; a break impacts the table or crosstab to which we apply the break. A section allows us to display multiple blocks of data on the same page, whereas a break does not allow us to display multiple blocks of data on the same page.

Sorts can be applied to the results that are displayed in a column or row to organize the order in which it should be displayed. We can apply sorts to any dimensions, measures, or details displayed in a table. Sorting dimensions and details helps us organize results chronologically, while sorting measures helps us see highest or lowest results at a glance. Sorts in WebI allow us to apply the following orders:

- **Default**: Referred to as the **natural order**. Depending on the type of data in the column or row, the results are sorted as follows:
    - Ascending numeric order for numeric data
    - Ascending chronological order for date
    - Ascending alphabetical order for alphanumeric data
- **Ascending**
- **Descending**
- **Custom**

Other features

Lets take a look at some of the features:

- **Input controls**: These are used for filtering and analyzing report data. We can define input controls using standard window controls such as text boxes and radio buttons. We can also define tables and charts as input controls. Input controls are specific to reports.
- **WebI conditional formatting**: This allows users to highlight results or change formatting based on data.
- **Data manager**: This allows a user to manage all of their data from a single place. It can be used to view, explore, and manage all of the queries in a document. It has the following features:
    - Insert, delete, update, change the data source, and view the results of the data provider
    - Create, modify, and delete merged dimensions
    - Create, modify, and delete local variables

- **Charts**: Data in SAP BusinessObjects WebI can also be represented in the form of a table, graph, or diagram. Different types of charts are supported in WebI and they can be inserted into existing or new reports. We can export these charts as Excel documents, as well as the `.pdf` files:

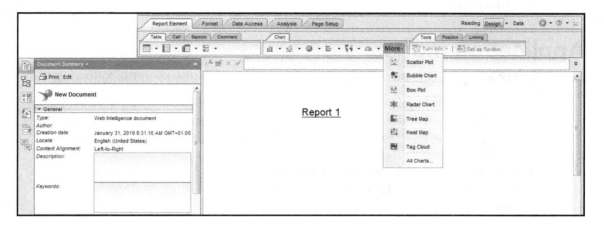

Let's see where we can use which type of chart:

Type	Usage
Bar charts	When we need to compare similar types of data. This can be either a stacked bar chart or a column bar chart.
Column charts	This is a vertical representation of values, and can be of various subtypes (three-dimensional column chart; stacked column chart; combined column line chart; column chart with two y axes).
Line charts	These are XY charts that display lines that connect plots together. Subtypes include area charts and line charts with two y axes.
Map charts	Values are displayed within nested rectangles that can be colored. Subtypes include heat maps and tree maps.
Pie charts	Data is displayed in a circular manner, with sectors splitting up the data. While circle represents the entirety of the data, a sector represents a part of it. Subtypes include donut charts and pie charts with slice depth.
Point charts	Its XY plot is represented by x and y coordinates. Subtypes include scatter plots, bubble charts, polar scatters, and polar bubble charts.
Spider charts	This is also known as a **radar chart**. It has several axes, each representing an analysis category.
Tag charts	Tag charts are mono-dimensional visualizations that represent data as words. The font of the word represents the relative weight of it in the dataset.

Waterfall	These are used to show the cumulative effect of the values of a measure, with each bar starting from the level of the previous one.
Box plot charts	These are mainly used to show outliers and are a graphical display of summaries based on the distribution of a dataset. For example the maximum, the minimum.

Application modes

SAP BusinessObjects WebI allows you to build and create documents in the following three modes:

- **Reading**: This is a display-only mode for existing reports. A user can track changes in the report and drill down on the data. This mode also allows you to do a text search.
- **Design**: In this mode, we can create, add, delete, and operate on the objects of a report. It allows you to use various conditional formatting and formulas, and also allows you to create variables.

Design mode operates from the server, so all the changes made to a report are done locally, in the server. In cases where we need to make a lot of changes to an existing report, it's always recommended that we make changes to the structure mode and then populate it with data.

- **Data**: This mode allows you to create new data sources and edit existing sources. If a query is used to pass data to reports, then we can create, edit, or make changes to the query in this mode as well:

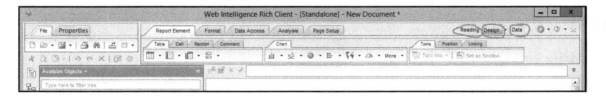

Now, let's try and see how can we use SAP BusinessObjects WebI to view, analyze, and create reports based on data about sales, products, and stores. The following exercise will make us familiar with the basic functions of SAP BusinessObjects WebI.

Creating a WebI document based on an existing Universe

Just like the previous exercises in this book, we have three different data sources: SAP BW query, Universe, and SAP HANA. Here, we will use the Universe as the data source and then look at how to use the SAP HANA view. The readers can then try this out with the SAP BW query (it's similar to the other two).

Let's create a WebI document based on an existing BEx query. In this case, we will pick up a sales query. Follow these steps to get started:

1. First, we need to make sure that **Preferred Startup Mode** for Design Studio is the SAP BusinessObjects BI platform. If it's not, then we need to change it and restart Design Studio.

    To change the startup mode, go to **Tools** I **Preferences**, in the **Application Design** I **Preferred Startup Mode** I **SAP Business Object BI platform** tab. Then, restart Design Studio.

2. Launch SAP BusinessObjects WebI for the BI launch pad:

SAP BusinessObjects
BI launch pad

Enter your user information, and click "Log On".
If you are unsure of your account information, contact your system administrator.

System: wdflbmt5073:6400
User Name:
Password:

Log On

Help

3. Log in with your user credentials.
4. In the BI launch pad, change your **Preferences** for **Web Intelligence**, to use the **Applet** version for both viewing and modifying documents:
    1. In the BI launch pad, choose **Preferences** | **Web Intelligence**. In the **View** screen area, choose the **Applet** radio button, as follows:

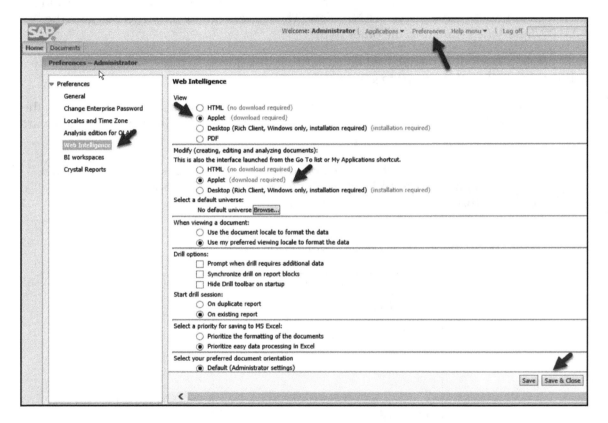

    2. In the **Modify** screen area, choose **Applet** | **Save & Close** | **OK**.

5. Launch SAP BusinessObjects WebI for the BI launch pad and go to the **My Applications** screen area. Choose the Web Intelligence icon. It might prompt you to do updates (Java) you can choose this option later to perform a security update:

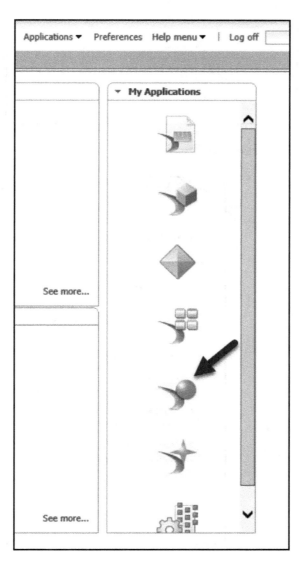

6. Choose New (Ctrl N) in Create a Web Intelligence document dialog box:

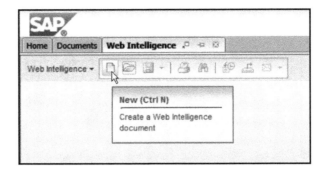

7. Then choose **Universe** | **OK**:

8. Select a Universe (in our case `eFashion`) dialog box. Double-click on the
    connection:

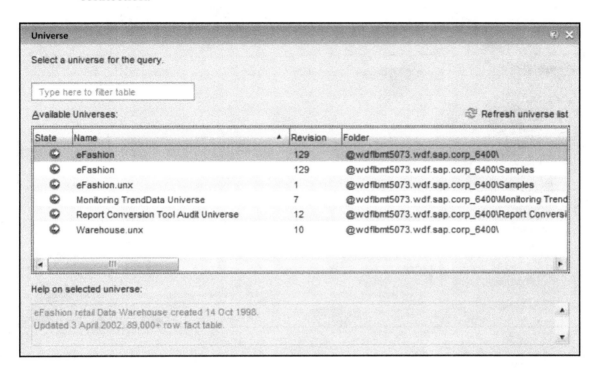

9. In the query panel, drag State, Store name to the **Result Objects** pane:

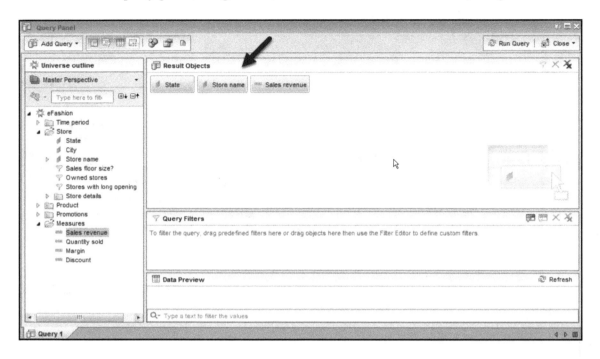

10. Drag `Sales revenue` from `Measures` into the **Result Objects** pane.

11. Choose **Run Query** | **Allow** | **OK** in the dialogue box (this is the document autosave and recovery dialog box):

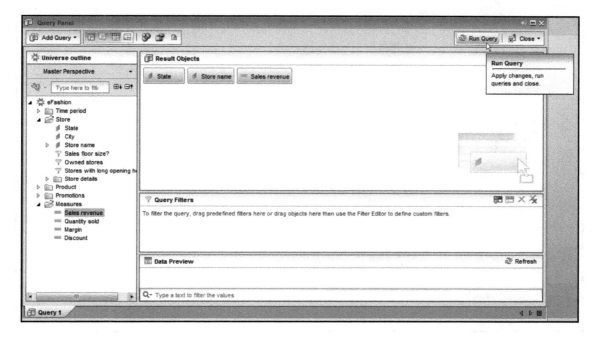

12. Go to **Page Setup** | **Rename Report** then give name to report as `sales revenue report`:

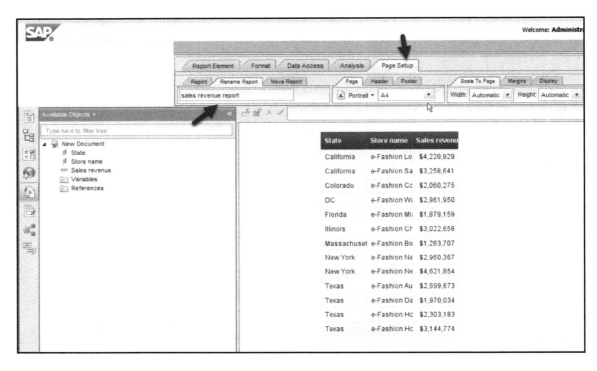

13. We can **Edit** the document we created previously to include a listing for the quantities that are sold by `Year` and `Month`, as follows:
    1. Choose **Data Access** | **Edit**:

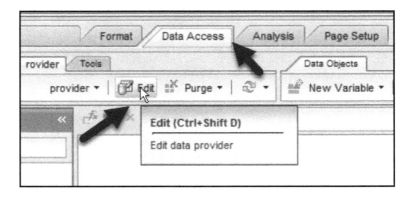

2. Drag `Year` and `Month` to the **Result Objects** pane. We will just drag and put `Quantity sold` to the **Result Objects** pane:

3. Choose **Run Query**. Drag the added objects into the **Report** panel.

14. Now, we can create a query filter so that we only display data for the `e_Fashion` XXX store. Choose any location that's available in your database:

1. Choose **Data Access | Edit**:

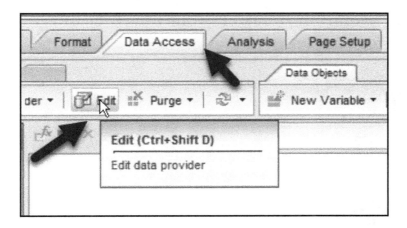

2. Drag `Store name` from the `Store` folder into the **Query Filters** pane:

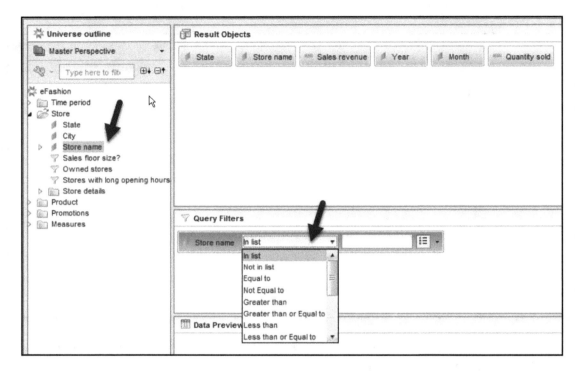

3. We need to enter search criteria, that is, XXX, and press the *Enter* key (the search is case-sensitive)
4. Choose `e_Fashion XXX` and add it to the **Selected Value(s)** pane
5. Choose **OK | Run Query**

15. We can also use filters and display the selected data for a particular year:
   1. Select the `Year` column and then select the **Analysis** tab
   2. Choose the arrow next to filter and click on **Add Filter** button:

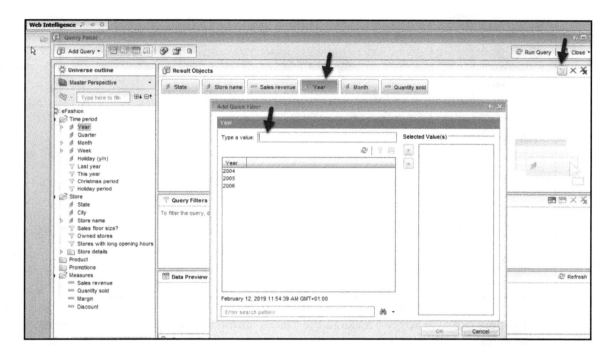

3. Double-click on the Year field

4. Select the year 2004, add it to the **Selected Value(s)** pane, and click **OK**:

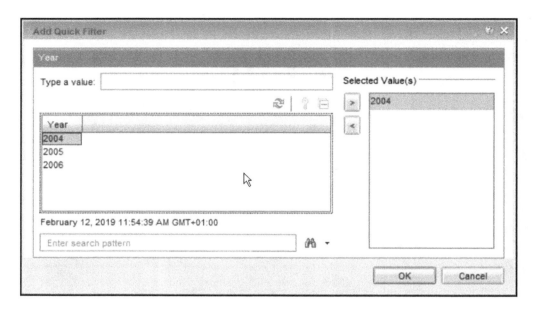

16. Readers can also apply breaks to the Year column and set the **Break** properties to merge duplicate values:

    1. Click on Year | **Analysis** | **Display**
    2. Choose the arrow next to the **Break** button and select **Add Break**
    3. Choose the arrow next to **Break** button and select **Manage Break**
    4. In the **Manage Break** window, choose the Year | **Duplicate Values** field, and then click **Merge** | **OK**

17. You can try applying other features, such as conditional formatting, sorts, and groups, and display the results in different orders and with various filters attached to them.

WebI document based on SAP HANA view

Now, we are going to create a WebI document based on an existing SAP HANA view. Here, we will use the same calculation. View AN_SALES (eFashion), which we used in previous exercises or use cases.

Steps 1-3 will be the same as for the previous implementation:

1. Choose **New | Create a Document** dialog box, and select **SAP HANA | OK**
2. Select the **HANA_OLAP** connection when the popup asks for the SAP HANA view
3. Select CALC_AN_SALES | **OK**
4. In the query panel, drag the State attribute (the DIM_GEOGRAPHY dimension) into the **Result Objects** pane
5. For the Store, proceed in a similar way
6. Drag the Amount sold measure into the **Result Objects** pane
7. Choose **Run Query | Allow | OK** for the dialogue box (that popup for document autosave and recovery dialog box)
8. Choose a name for your report, for example, Demo Sales_HANA report
9. Just like the preceding use case, we can apply various conditional formatting, sorts, groups, and display the results in various orders and with various filters
10. You can also try all of the filtering features and other features that are available to present the result in a different order and with different criteria

Through these steps, we have created a WebI document based on SAP HANA view and BO Universe and learned how to create an analytical application using BO Universe and SAP HANA view. A WebI document can also be created using the BW BEx query as the data source in a similar fashion. I leave this as an exercise for you.

Summary

In this chapter, we became familiar with SAP BusinessObjects WebI. We learned how to create a SAP BusinessObjects WebI document and how to use features like query, report, and analyze. We also discussed features like breaks, WebI calculation, groups, and the data manager in WebI. Finally, we concluded this chapter with a step-by-step guide on how to create WebI documents using various data sources.

In the next chapter, we will learn how to create a report in SAP Crystal Report for Enterprise. We will explore various toolbars and report elements. We will also introduce you to the action architecture and how to navigate further into the information that's provided by BI tools. We will close this chapter with a use case, where we will create a report.

5
SAP BusinessObject Crystal Reports

In this chapter, we'll learn how to create a report in SAP Crystal Reports for Enterprise. We'll explore various toolbars and report elements that are available. We'll also introduce the Insight to Action architecture and how to navigate further into the information that's provided in BI tools. We'll close this chapter with a use case where we'll create a report.

In this chapter, we'll cover the following topics:

- Introduction to SAP Crystal Reports
- Creating a report in SAP Crystal Reports

Introduction to SAP Crystal Reports

SAP Crystal Reports allows us to create richly formatted and dynamic reports from any data sources, which can then be delivered in many formats and in multiple languages. With SAP Crystal Reports, we can turn any data source into interactive, actionable information that can be accessed online or offline from portals and from mobile devices or applications.

SAP Crystal Reports for the Enterprise design environment has the following basic functionalities:

- Create new, open, and save
- Print and export
- Undo and redo
- Cut, copy, and paste
- Format painter

Toolbars in SAP Crystal Reports for Enterprise

There are three different toolbars in SAP Crystal Reports for Enterprise, as shown in the following screenshot:

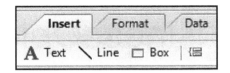

Let's learn what we can do with these toolbars:

- **Insert**: With this tool, you can insert new elements into our report such as textboxes, groups, and charts.
- **Format**: With this tool, you can find all of the available options for changing the format of an element such as font size, font type, colors, and alignment of the elements
- **Data**: This tool allows you to edit the query, define sorts, and add interactive filters

From the **Data Explorer** panel, we can insert, modify, or delete objects in our report. When we create a new report or open an existing report, the **Data Explorer** side panel opens adjacent to the report canvas. The objects that we add in the query panel are stored in **Data Explorer**, where they can be added to the report. The following list mentions some possible objects:

- **Result Objects**
- **Formulas**
- **Parameters**
- **Running Totals**
- **Predefined Objects**

The **Outline** panel shows the content of the report in a tree view. The root node is the report itself, while the first-level nodes represent the sections of the report. Within each section, the report's objects and elements are listed. You can modify these objects using the context menu:

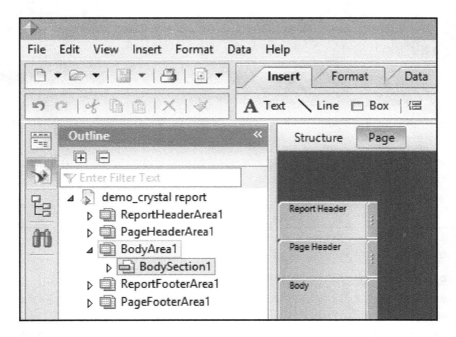

The **Group Tree** panel shows a tree view of groups and subgroups in the report. Any item you select in **Group Tree** is selected on the report canvas.

Use the **Search** side panel to search the report for any specific value. Type a word or phrase into the textbox and, on the keyboard, press the *Enter* key. The search results appear in the side panel.

The report layout is divided into various sections. Each section has its own properties, which are used in different ways. The following screenshot shows the structure of a report:

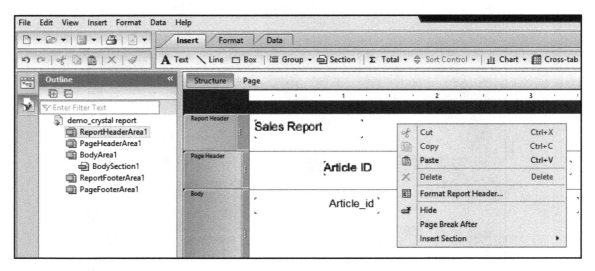

It has the following area:

- **Report Header**: We use this for the report title and other information that we want to appear at the beginning of the report. It can also be used for charts and cross tabs that include data for the entire report.
- **Page Header**: This enables us to put information that we want to appear at the top of each page such as chapter names and the name of documents.
- **Body**: We use this for the body of the report. This is printed once for the record. Most of the report data will appear in this section.
- **Report Footer**: We use this area for displaying information that we want to appear at the end of the report, such as grand totals, as well as for charts or cross tabs that include data for the entire report.
- **Page Footer**: With this, we can display the page numbers and other information that we want to appear on the bottom of each page. If we added a group to the report, the program would create two additional sections:
  - **Group Header**: This holds the group name objects. We can use this to display charts or cross tabs that include data that's specific to the group. It's printed once at the beginning of a group.
  - **Group Footer**: This contains a summary value, if any, and can be used to display charts or cross tabs. It's printed once, at the end of a group.

The report element has the following elements:

- **Result Objects**: These are the objects that display data from the data source. Most of the data that's displayed on a report is from result objects.
- **Formulas**: There are situations where the data source stores only the order dates and ship dates for orders. However, we also need to display the number of days it takes to ship the order. In this case, we can create a formula that'll calculate the number of days between ordering and shipping.
- **Parameters**: This allows you to filter report data for specific users. For example, a sales report can have region as a parameter.
- **Running Totals**: To display a total that evaluates each record and provides a running sum of all of the values in an object (or all of the values in a certain set of values), a running total element is created and placed in the report.
- **Predefined Objects**: Predefined objects include **Page Number**, **Record Number**, **Group Number**, **Print Date**, and **Total Page Count**. Use the commands in the **Predefined Objects** area of the **Data Explorer** side panel to add predefined objects to your report.
- **Text Elements**: These are mostly used to hold text, but they can also hold result objects to create custom form letters and more.
- **Picture**: This allows us to include images/pictures in reports, for example, a company logo.

Data sources for SAP Crystal Reports

Crystal Reports supports connections to the following data sources. However, prior to connecting to the following data sources, we would be required to connect to an SAP BI platform first:

- **SAP BEx Query**
- **Analysis View**
- **Relational Connection**
- **Universe**

Once we've chosen the data source, the **Edit Query** panel appears. We can now select elements to include in our query. However, please keep in mind that if we connect to an analysis view, the **Query** panel won't appear because analysis views contain predesigned queries. In this case, the report canvas will appear instead.

Data grouping and sorting

We can group data and sort it. Grouped data is data that's sorted and separated into meaningful groups, for example, a customer list may be grouped by region. In a sales report, a group might consist of all orders that are placed by a particular customer or orders that are generated by a particular sales representative or for a particular region.

Sort and group direction options are made available when we have the data grouped:

- **Ascending order**: This allows you to sort your data from smallest to largest. It sorts the records in ascending order and then begins a new group whenever the value changes.
- **Descending order**: This allows you to sort your data from largest to smallest. It sorts the records in descending order and then begins a new group whenever the value changes.
- **Specified order**: This is customized as per our needs. With the help of specified orders, we can place each record into the customer group that we've specified and leave the records in each group in their original order. This means that we can sort them in ascending or descending order, depending on how we want to do things.

When we sort, we have the sort direction (ascending or descending), and the object we want the sort to be based on (sort object). Sort objects let you determine the order in which data appears on your report. Almost any object can be used for sorting, including formulas. An object's data type determines how the data from that object is sorted. In single object sorting, all of the records that are used in the report are sorted based on the values in a single object. Sorting an inventory report by stock number or sorting a customer list by customer number are examples of single object sorts. With multiple object sorts, Crystal Reports first sorts the records based on the values in the first object that's selected, putting them in ascending or descending order, as specified. If two or more records have a matching object value in the first sort object, the matching records are sorted by the value in the second sort object. For example, if you choose to sort first by country and then by region, both in ascending order, the report would appear with countries listed in alphabetic order and regions within each country listed in alphabetic order. Any other objects, such as the postal codes within each region, would remain unsorted.

Creating a report in SAP Crystal Reports

Whenever we create a new report, we have three options in terms of data sources that we can choose from (BW query, Universe, and SAP HANA view). Let's look at how we can create a report in SAP Crystal Reports. We can use any of the three different data sources, just like in the previous exercises of this book—BW query, Universe, and SAP HANA view. We'll see the steps for two (using BW query or relational database and SAP HANA view) of these and leave the third one as an exercise for the readers.

We'll start by using BW query as a data source. The steps for this exercise are as follows:

1. Launch SAP Crystal Reports:

2. Create a new server connection. Go to **File** | **Log On To Server**:

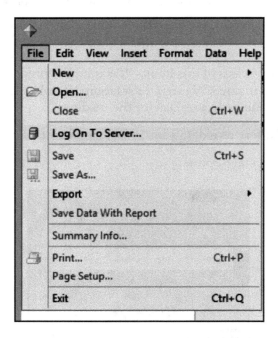

3. After that, the **Connect To Server** dialog box will appear (provide details) and click on **OK**:

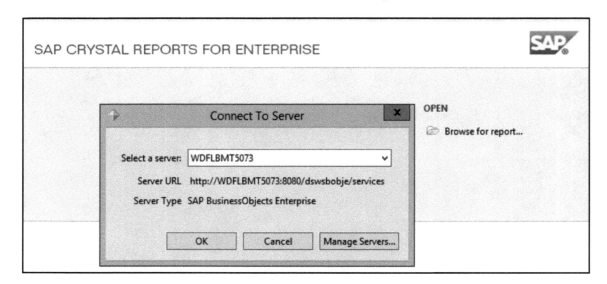

4. Provide the credentials that are provided by your administrator (**User Name** and **Password**):

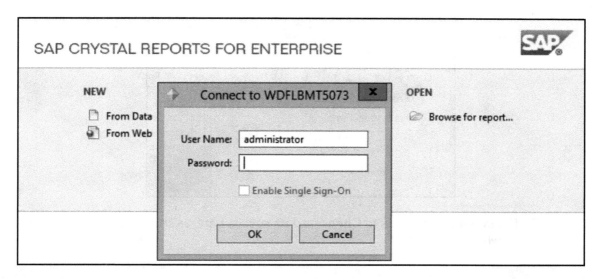

5. Click on **Test connection**. On successful connection, a message popup at the bottom-left of your screenshot will appear, confirming the successful connection:

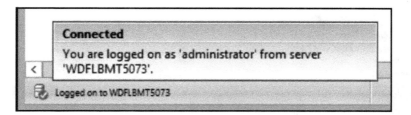

6. Choose the data source from which we would like to create the report. Choose **From Data Source**, as shown in the following screenshot:

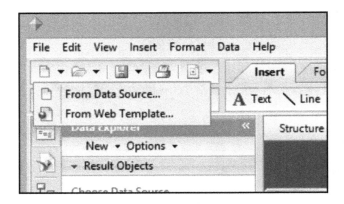

7. The system will ask us to **Choose a data source type**, as shown follows. Click on **Browse Repository**:

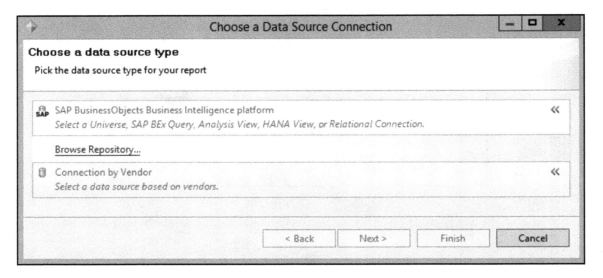

8. We can either choose **Universe** or **Relational Connection** (for BW and SAP HANA). Here, we choose **Relational Connection**, as follows:

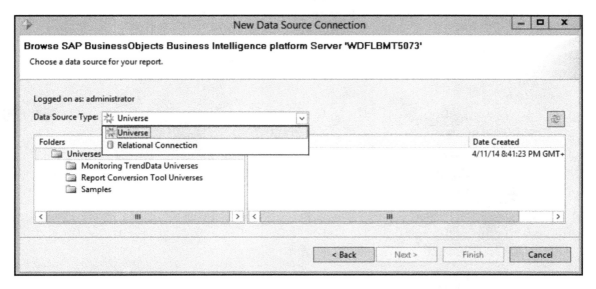

9. From the following screenshot, we can see that, the system shows all of the connections within **Relational Connection**. We'll use **efashion** (since we downloaded the files for `efashion` in `Chapter 1`, *Overview of SAP BusinessObject Business Intelligence 4.2*):

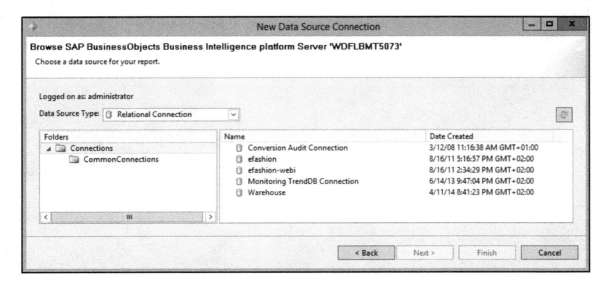

10. We can select the table that we would like to link to our reports. We can select as many tables as we want as shown in the following:

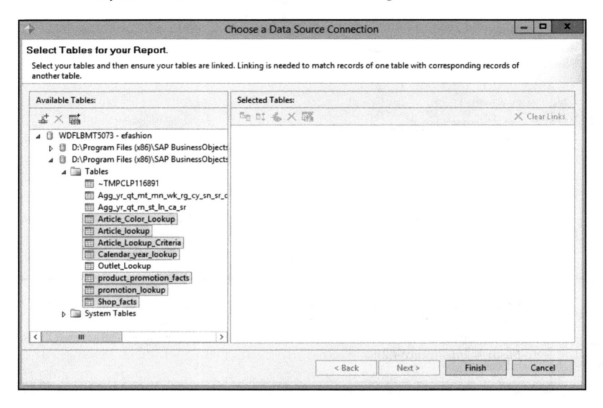

11. Once we click on **Finish** after selecting the tables, we can link (join) the tables, as follows:

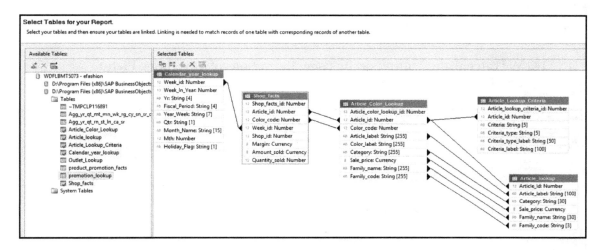

12. A blank structure will appear, as shown in the following screenshot. We can drag the various fields of tables and put them into different areas (**Report Header**, **Page Header**, and so on):

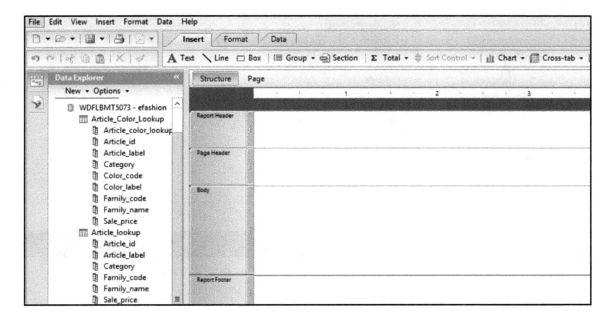

13. Drag the objects from the left-hand side into different sections (**Report Header** and **Report Footer**):

- `Sale_price`
- `Artical_id`
- `Color_code`

14. We can enhance our report by using the options of **Text**, **Line**, **Picture**, and **Cross-tab** to name a few:

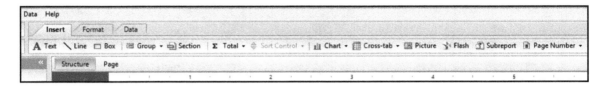

15. We'll add some text to our report, `Sales Report 2019`:

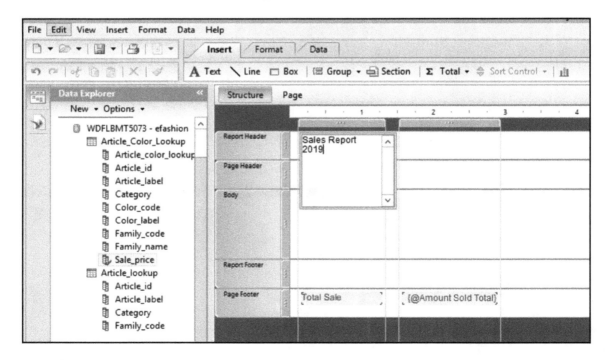

16. We also want to create a formula for total sales based on the amount sold. We used the standard features, as shown in the following screenshot:

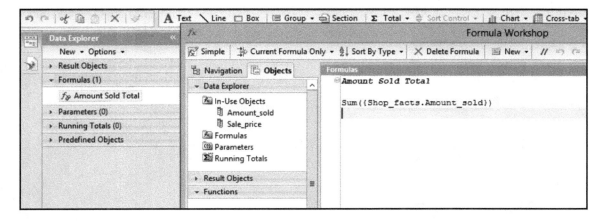

We used `Sum` to add new elements to our group to show the amount sold in total.

17. You can drag and drop various fields onto the structure and then create the report structure however you want:

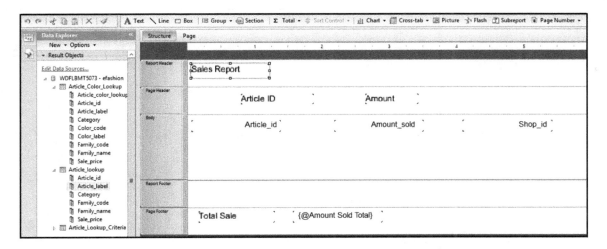

18. You can always look at the **Page** tab and see how it will look:

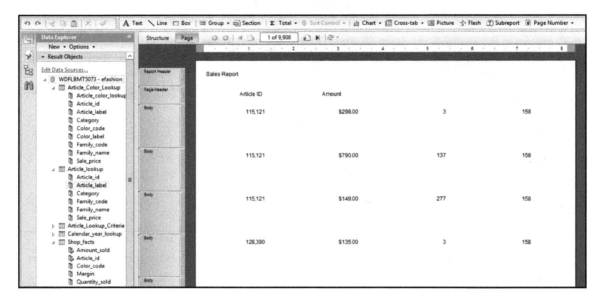

19. Save the report to the BI platform server. Choose **File** | **Save**:

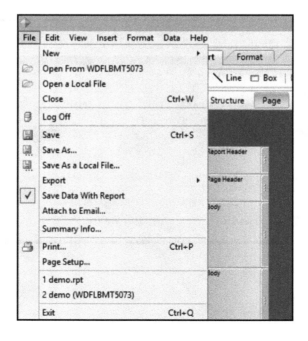

20. Choose **All Folders | My Folders | My Favorites**:

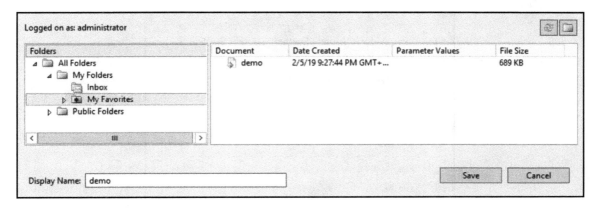

21. Give it a name and **Save** it. This will be the name that's used automatically for the report title.
22. In the **Report Contains Saved Data** dialog box, choose **Save with Data**:

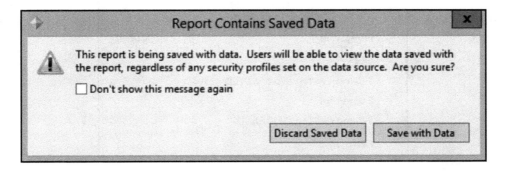

23. Go to **File** | **Export** | **PDF**:

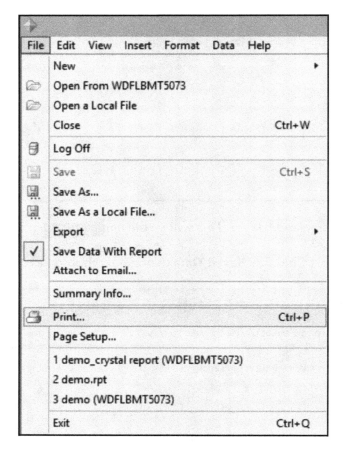

24. In the **Export Options - PDF** dialog box, ensure that the **All pages** radio button is selected and choose **OK.** In the **Export Destination** dialog box, choose **To Application**. The PDF file will open automatically:

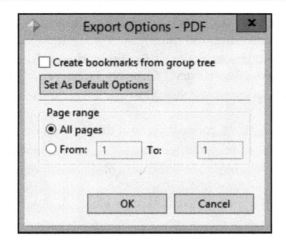

25. Review the PDF file and, to close the Adobe Reader application, choose **File** | **Exit**.

26. We can make our report well-formatted and aligned by adjusting the color and layout of it. We can do this by using features such as report header and footer. I leave this for the reader to explore.

27. The report that we've created can now be viewed in the BI launchpad.

Creating the report with SAP HANA view as a data source

Now, let's create the report with SAP HANA view as the data source. We'll use the same calculation view that we used in our previous exercises (the CALC_AN_SALES view). The steps for this exercise are as follows:

1. Launch SAP Crystal Reports.

2. Create a new server connection. Go to **File** | **Log On To Server** | **Connect To Server** | **OK**. Then, provide the credentials that are provided by your administrator (**User Name** and **Password**).

3. Click on **Test connection.** Enter your password and click **OK**.

4. Create a new report, say, `z_demo_crystal_report_HANA`, showing the year, state, city, sales revenue, and margin.

5. Choose **New** | **Data source type** | **BusinessObjects Intelligence Platform** | **Browse Repository** | **Connect To Server** | **OK.**

6. Select the new data source connection and then choose **SAP HANA** view as the data source.

7. Choose the `HANA_OLAP` connection, and then select **Next**.

8. Go to the `efashion` folder, select `CALC_AN_SALES`, and then click **OK**.

9. Drag the objects from the left-hand side of the result objects into the **Query** panel:
   - `YR`
   - `State`
   - `Store`
   - `Amount sold`
   - `Margin`

The next steps are the same ones that we used when we used the BEx query as a data source:

1. Check the **Generate** checkbox and select **Finish**.

2. Go to **Insert**, choose the **Group** button, and mark the **Ascending** radio button for **Calendar year** (you can now sort how you want).

3. Add new elements to our group to show the number of cities and total sales revenue. For that, go to the **Insert** tab and click the **Total** button. Define the new total, whether it be city, distinct count, sum of, or sales revenue.

4. Save the report to the BI platform server:
   1. Choose **File** | **Save**.
   2. Choose **All Folders** | **My Folders** | **My Favorites**.
   3. Give it a name and save it. This will be the name that's used automatically for the report title.
   4. In the **Report Contains Saved Data** dialog box, choose **Save with Data**.
   5. Choose **File** | **Export** | **PDF**.
   6. In the **Export Options - PDF** dialog box, ensure that the **All pages** radio button is selected, and then click **OK**. In the **Export Destination** dialog box, choose **To Application**. The PDF file will open automatically.
   7. Review the PDF file and, to close the Adobe Reader application, choose **File** | **Exit**.

5. We can make our report well-formatted and aligned by adjusting the color and layout of it. We can do this by using features such as report header and footer. I leave this for the reader to explore.

6. The report that we've created can now be viewed in the BI launchpad.

Insight to Action

Insight to Action provides additional functionality so that you can navigate/drill further into the information that's provided in BI tools such as Crystal Reports and Dashboards (formerly known as **Xcelsius**). Using the Insight to Action framework, an action in a BI document can take us to the next logical step in a business process with context, hence allowing us to access related data in a SAP system and launch an internet URL or another document.

The architecture of Insight to Action consists of the following elements:

- BI client
- BI platform
- I2A (Insight to Action) web services
- Crystal Reports
- Xcelsius

These elements are shown in the following diagram:

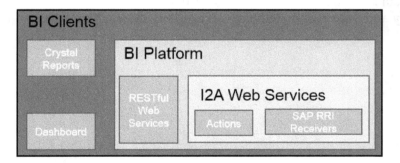

Web services are hosted to communicate between the actions that are provided, where SAP **Report to Report Interface** (**RRI**) **Receivers** are built inside SAP NetWeaver BW and actions are external data elements. Actions are configured for the reports or dashboards so that they can navigate to external data elements. SAP RRI Actions are configured on SAP systems and are supported only on reports that are based on BEx queries. When invoking an action from a report object, the data for the object, as well as the entire row of data, is passed to the RRI action. RRI actions can use this data in whichever way has been configured and process that data. Enable Actions in your Crystal Report to use the RRI actions that have been defined for the query in the SAP System. To do so, right-click on the relevant object and choose **Enable Action**. Once the RRI actions have been enabled, an icon will appear to the right-hand side of the enabled objects when you hover over them. Clicking this icon will show the list of RRI actions that have been configured in the SAP system. The relevant BEx query will then open. This query shows the data that was included when the action was invoked.

Summary

In this chapter, we got a general overview of SAP Crystal Reports. We learned how to create a report in SAP Crystal Reports for Enterprise. We also explored the various toolbars and report elements that are available. We introduced the Insight to Action architecture and how to navigate further into the information that's provided in BI tools.

In the next chapter, we'll learn about SAP Lumira. We'll learn how to visualize and manipulate data using a SAP Lumira Storyboard and learn how the self-service approach to data discovery and information delivery can be easily done with the tool.

6
SAP BusinessObject SAP Lumira

In this chapter, we will learn how to visualize and manipulate data using a SAP Lumira storyboard. We will also learn how we can use the self-service approach to perform data discovery and information delivery.

We will cover the following topics:

- Introduction to SAP Lumira
- Use cases for Lumira
- Visualization using Lumira
- Charts and data sharing

Introduction to SAP Lumira

SAP Lumira is a self-service data manipulation, visualization, and story creation tool that can connect to one or more data sources to create datasets. These datasets come from one or multiple sources and can be enhanced with new measures, hierarchies, and created columns (also called **custom columns**).

Lumira has a wide range of graphical charts and tables, which enables end users to visualize their data in a more interactive fashion. Users can create stories that provide a graphical narrative to describe their data, which is done by grouping charts together on boards to create presentation style dashboards. By adding images and text, we can annotate and add presentation details.

The installation of SAP Lumira is done locally and works well with both remote and local data. It allows us to save the charts that have been built on the datasets. These can then be printed or sent via email if required. It is possible to publish these datasets on **SAP HANA**, **SAP BEx**, **SAP Lumira Cloud**, **SAP Lumira Server**, and **SAP StreamWork activities**. The default file format for datasets and charts that are created in SAP Lumira is `.lums`. `*.lums` contains information such as the data source connection, data definition, visualization, and the data itself.

Use cases for Lumira

Since SAP Lumira delivers insights via its self-service approach, your business does not have to wait for IT professionals to create a predefined query or a report each time a new insight is required (by the business). This also means that the IT team will have no additional workload and therefore the business can avoid having to create additional, silo infrastructures across organizations to support the increased demand for data-driven visualization. SAP Lumira can connect to the SAP BusinessObjects BI platform or SAP Crystal Server software.

The use cases for Lumira are as follows:

- Self-service data insights
- Data discovery functionality for existing data, metadata, and personal sources
- It does not require you to predefine or create custom queries and reports
- It focuses on its core mission of delivering information to the business on time, without compromising on governance and security
- It has a security model and one BI platform

SAP Lumira supports the following data sources:

- Microsoft Excel
- CSV files
- SAP HANA
- SAP BW data exposed as views in SAP HANA
- SAP BusinessObjects Universe
- Querying with **Structured Query Language** (**SQL**)

Depending on your data source, data can be adapted before acquisition to include or remove columns, attributes, measures, or SAP HANA variables and input parameters. For certain data sources we have other options, such as data formatting, column naming and trimming, and specifying column name prefixes. We can also edit a data source that has been acquired. We can add or remove columns, attributes, measures, and variables from the original data source.

 Machine capacity limits the maximum number of cells that can be acquired when data is acquired for local manipulation.

Data preparation

In the **Data** panel, there's raw data, and most of it has no formatting whatsoever. This cannot be easily interpreted by business users. Due to this, before creating the charts to visualize our data, we would need to clean it up so as to make it presentable and understandable. Cleaning the data can be done in the **Grid** or **Facets** view. To the right of the **Data** panel, we have the data editing panel, which allows us to perform column management tasks, such as column duplication, splitting, renaming, and removing. Similarly, row-level editing tasks such as setting values to lowercase, finding and replacing, adding or trimming text, and adding formulas can be performed. Editing tasks can be applied to selected columns or to all of them.

Prepare view

We use the **Prepare** view to view, clean, and prepare our data before creating charts. This view displays the data from the connected data source. In this section, we look at the various panels that are underneath this view.

Date panel

The **Date** panel is used to view data, which can then be displayed as columns (when we choose the **Grid** view) or as **Facets** (when we choose the **Facets** view). We can apply the following column values by clicking the arrow in the column headers:

- **Filters**
- **Sort**
- **Rename**

- Merge
- Delete
- Merger
- Hide

These options are shown in the following screenshot:

Object Picker and column data manipulation panel

The **Measures** and **Attributes** that are detected by SAP Lumira are listed here. We can also edit or define new measures and create time and geography hierarchies. The following objects can be found in the dataset:

- **Measures:** When we need to combine different columns, we use a measure to get the calculated result. It is automatically detected and listed.

- **Hierarchies**: This allows us to reference more than one related column in our dataset. These columns have hierarchical relationships.

- **Attributes**: Maps to columns in the dataset.

- **Inferred Attributes**: These are the columns that are created based on geographical information or time (if they are available to SAP).

The column data manipulation panel contains data manipulation tools that can be applied to a selected cell or column so that you can edit a test, convert values, create new columns with formulas, and rename, duplicate, and remove columns.

Data manipulation panel

This panel contains editing tools that allow us to edit and format values both at the column and row level for a column that's been selected in the **Data** view. Depending on the data type of the selected column, we can perform the following activities:

- Duplicate, rename, and remove columns
- Create columns with formulas
- Find, replace, and change string values

- Convert, trim, and group values
- Fill in prefixes and suffixes
- Edit within text strings

Data editing and cleaning panel

The data editing and cleaning panel allows us to edit and format the values in a column. The editor is a collapsible vertical sidebar that contains data manipulation tools. We can use the editor in either the **Grid** or **Facets** view, and implement the following editing options:

- **Duplicate**: Used for duplicating a selected column to create a new one.
- **Rename**: Used for renaming an existing column.
- **Remove**: Used to remove an existing column.
- **Split**: This helps us with creating a new column with string values, which appear after a defined split point. The split can be, for example, a punctuation mark, a comma, or a text string.
- **Create**: Used for creating a new column for number and date types that apply a function to values.
- **Set case**: This is used in the case where we need to change the string values to either lower or upper case.
- **Find and replace:** This is used when we need to find a string and replace it with a new string.
- **Fill**: This option is used to specify a character so that we can either prefix or suffix a string to a defined character length.
- **Convert**: With the convert edit tool, we can convert a column into text, a number, or data.
- **Trim**: This allows us to remove characters after or before a specific punctuation mark or character.
- **Grouping**: When we need to create a new column in which we can create a new group of rows, we can use the grouping option.

The preceding options can be seen in the following screenshot:

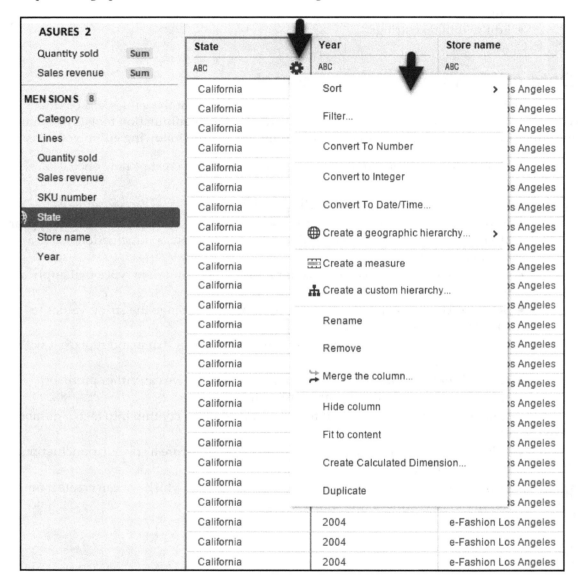

Data filtering in columns and charts

To limit the values that are displayed in charts, we can use a filter to put a restriction on the dataset. For example, if our chart shows revenue for products sold in the years between 2000 and 2018 and we want to only see revenue for the years 2008 to 2018, we can create a filter on the dimension **Year** to limit the values that are shown in this period. Each filter that's created in a column appears as an entry in the global filters bar at the top of the **Data** panel. We can edit the filter directly from the **Filter** bar. Broadly speaking, we have two options based on the scope of filters:

- **Dataset filter**: With this filter, we can define a filter on a column that's applied to both the data and the charts that use the column.
- **Visualization level filter**: With this filter, we can define a filter on a chart that's only been applied to the chart. The filter will have no effect on the data at the dataset level.

Filter panel

Filters are defined in the **Filter** panel, which is accessible from the drop-down menu for a column header, or from the **Filter** category in the **Chart Feeder** panel. Please note that a filter that's defined on a chart only applies to the chart. The following filter options are available in the **Filter** panel for text-based data:

- **Search Field**: This allows us to type in one or more characters of a column value so that we can search and display the value.
- **All Values:** All unique values for the column are listed with the count of occurrence for each value.
- **Add, remove, remove all:** This option allows you to add a value to the filter, remove a value from the filter, or remove all values from the **Filtered Values** panel.
- **Filtered Values:** Selected values to filter.
- **Keep Only:** This option is used to retain the values that are in the **Filtered Values** panel of the column. All other values in the column do not appear in the column or dimension.
- **Exclude Values:** This is used to include all values in the column or dimension, except for the values in the **Filtered Values** panel. We define a filter so that we can exclude certain values.

The preceding options can be seen in the following screenshot:

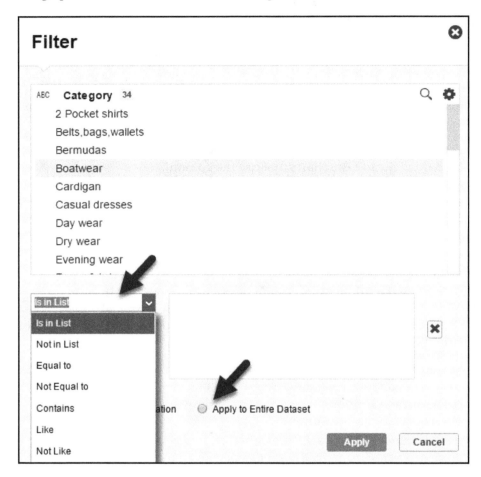

Number and date formatting

The following display options are available for columns that are of the number and data type:

Display option	Description
Use a scientific number format	Uses a decimal point separator
Use a 1,000 separator	Uses a comma separator
Number of decimals	Specifies the number of decimal places for the column values
Data display formats (date type only)	Selects a date format

Visualization and storyboards

With SAP Lumira, we can combine our visualizations into storyboards so that we can organize our data in a meaningful way. Storyboards allow users to group their created visualizations through the use of a wide range of storage control options. These can change the format and feel of the storyboard to help increase its usability. Storyboards can be created in the **Compose** tab of SAP Lumira.

We can use the **Visualize** tab to create charts from a wide selection of chart families. The **Visualize** tab uses the **Object Picker** panel, which contains the **Measures** and **Attributes** that were defined in the dataset, a **chart body** panel to visualize the chart, and the **Chart Feeder** panel:

Visualization method	Method	Description
Chart Feeder panel	By activating the **Chart Feeder** panel and dragging attributes and measures to the **Chart Feeder** panel.	The **Chart Feeder** panel provides a structured method to build a chart. We can drag measures and objects to the indicated categories, as well as add calculations, sort and rank, measures, and define filters.

Visualizations are limited to 10,000 data points in this release.

The following categories and options are available in the **Chart Feeder** panel:

Category	Description	Options
Measures	• They are predefined and available in the **Semantic** panel • Every chart must have at least one measure • If multiple measures are present, different colors are used to represent the measures	• Sorting is possible (ascending or descending) • Adding a calculation is also possible; therefore, we can choose a predefined calculation • Ranking values is also possible by selecting the dimension in the chart
Dimensions	Multiple attributes can be added in **Chart Feeder**.	• The color legend can be used for attributes • Axis labels are also available, depending on the type of chart
Trellis	Attributes can be added.	N/A
Filter	We can filter the dimensions either on a single value of the dimension or choose multiple values.	N/A

Chart types in SAP Lumira

SAP Lumira offers multiple chart types that you can choose from for your visualization. Various chart families are available so that we can visualize our data in the way we want it to be visualized. The following table lists the various chart types that are available:

Type of data analysis	Used for	Options (charts)
Comparison	When we need to visualize the difference between values or simply show a comparison of the categorical division of measures.	• Bar chart (vertical/horizontal) • Bar chart with two y axes • Surface chart • Radar chart (single/multiple)
Percentage	Showing the percentage of parts of a whole or to show a value as a ratio of the whole.	• Pie (single/multiple) • Tree map • 100% stacked bar chart (vertical/horizontal)
Correlation	When we want to visualize the relationship between values or compare multiple measure values.	• Scatter chart • Bubble chart
Geographical	Showing a map of a country in the analysis.	• Geographical bubble chart • Geo choropleth chart • Geo pie chart

Trend	To show a trend in the data values, especially for dimensions that are time bound (such as year/month).	• Line chart • Line chart with two *y* axes • Multibar chart • Multiline chart with multiple measures

In SAP Lumira, we can also use predictive calculation and add various pieces of information to our charts. It supports two types of predictive analysis:

- **Forecast**: This allows us to predict how data may behave in a defined future period. Depending on the chart we use, the forecasted data is displayed as bars or a colored line.
- **Linear regression**: With this form of predictive analysis, we can see how data is distributed around our actual data to give us a generalized trend over time. Depending on the type of chart we use, the regression is displayed as bars or a line that's superimposed over the existing chart plots.

> Forecasting is based on the **Triple Exponential Smoothing** algorithm, which predicts based on a single fixed time period.

Sharing the charts, stories, and datasets

The stories, charts, and datasets that we create can be shared in SAP Lumira in various ways. In this section, we will go over a few of the methods.

Sharing charts

Let's refer to the following methods that we can use to share charts:

Method	Description
Sending charts by email	We can automatically attach our charts to an email message and send them to collaborators.
Saving the document on filesystems	We can save our documents/charts and data as `.lums` documents.
Printing our charts	We can print the charts as Adobe PDF files.
SAP Lumira Cloud	We can save our documents to SAP Lumira Cloud directly and have regular refreshes and save actions scheduled.

Sharing stories

Let's refer to the following methods that we can use to share stories:

Method	Description
SAP Lumira Cloud	We can publish (via your SAP Lumira Cloud account) our stories to the SAP Lumira Cloud and view them there.

 Stories cannot be edited on Lumira Cloud, but updated versions can be republished from SAP Lumira.

Sharing datasets

Let's refer to the following methods that we can use to share datasets:

Method	Description
Export	We can save a dataset as a CSV file or a Microsoft Excel file.
Publish to SAP HANA	We can publish a dataset to SAP HANA as a new analytic view.
Publish to SAP BEx	A dataset can be published to SAP BEx.
Publish to SAP StreamWork	We can publish documents to SAP StreamWork.
Publish to SAP Lumira Cloud	We can publish (via your SAP Lumira Cloud account) a dataset to SAP Lumira Cloud so that we can store documents and collaborate with colleagues so that they can work on our datasets.

While sharing or exporting our datasets, we have to follow some restrictions, as follows:

- Hidden and visible objects are exported
- A filter has no impact, so the export is done without taking filters into consideration
- Similarly, sorting is not taken into account
- If columns are referenced multiple times, they will be exported multiple times

Sending charts by email

SAP Lumira allows us to send our charts as graphical file attachments in our default mail program. If a chart is of the table type, then can be attached to an email as a Microsoft Excel file attachment, and not as a graphical file:

Method	Description
Directly	You can send your charts directly from charts.
Selective	You can send your charts by selecting a saved chart in the share panel.

Introduction to SAP Lumira Cloud

SAP Lumira Cloud is a SaaS hosted by SAP. SAP Lumira acquires data, connects to sources, takes this data to the analyst, and then the analyst transforms the data. Using the Java connector, SAP Lumira can connect to SAP **Enterprise Resource Planning (ERP)**, **Central Component (ECC)**, and any **Java Database Connectivity (JDBC)** source.

It can connect to SAP HANA when it's both online (data is not saved to your desktop) and offline (data is saved to your desktop and can be used locally). The most important features of SAP Lumira Cloud are as follows:

- It's built on and optimized for SAP HANA
- It's hosted and managed by SAP
- It has the same SAP identification as the SAP community network
- It uses HTML5 technology to provide an optimized mobile device experience
- Data can be published from SAP Lumira desktop to SAP Lumira Cloud or uploaded from Microsoft Excel documents

Creating a SAP Lumira visualization

We can create a SAP Lumira visualization by using the SAP Lumira reporting tool. The three different sources of data can be used with this tool: BW query, Universe, and SAP HANA view. In this section, we will present a story about the revenue of our sample company's data (eFashion).

We will look at how we can create visualizations using a Universe (eFashion) and using SAP BW query as a data source. You can try this yourself by using SAP HANA for your data source visualizations.

Creating a Lumira report based on the eFashion packages and Universe

For this exercise, we will use some sample `eFashion` Universe data, which is available at : `https://wiki.scn.sap.com/wiki/display/BOBJ/eFashion+on+HANA`.

Follow these steps to learn how to create a Lumira report based on Universe data:

1. Launch SAP Lumira from your desktop.
2. Create a new report in SAP Lumira. Choose **File** | **New** | **Create a new dataset**, as shown in the following screenshot:

3. Choose **SAP Universe Query Panel** and then click **Next**:

4. The system may prompt you to **Update Extensions** (depending on what you have chosen). I had the following prompt:

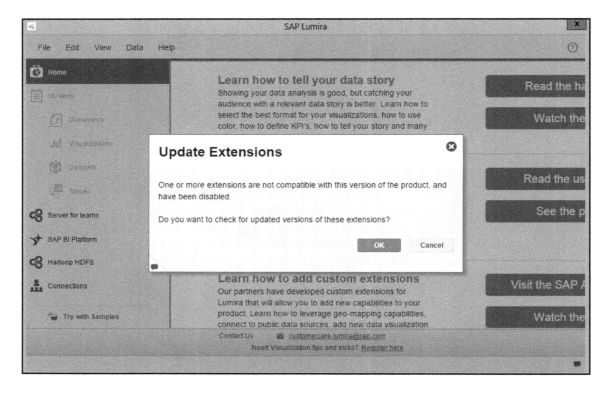

5. Choose **OK**. After a few minutes, the extensions will have been updated, and you will get the following pop-up message, asking you to restart the Lumira client:

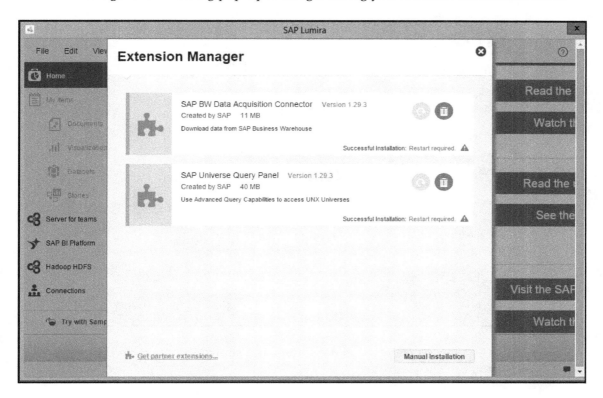

6. After this has been restarted, you will be asked for your **Universe credentials**. Provide all the necessary details and click on **Next**:

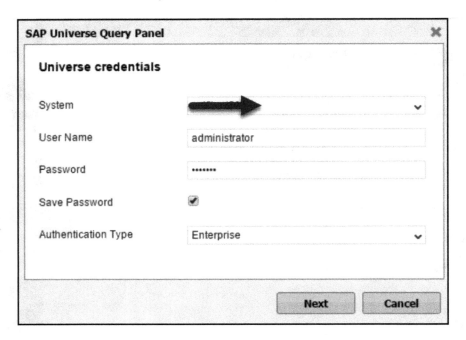

You will be connected to the system and shown the available Universes that you can choose from.

7. Choose the Universe called `eFashion`. Name the dataset `Lumira Exercise with Universe`, as follows:

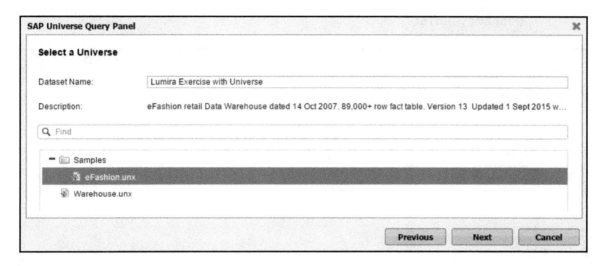

8. Add the following dimensions and measures to the results panel by dragging them from the navigation panel to the **Result Objects for Query #1** panel: Year, State, City, Store name, Category, Lines, SKU number, Sales revenue, Quantity sold:

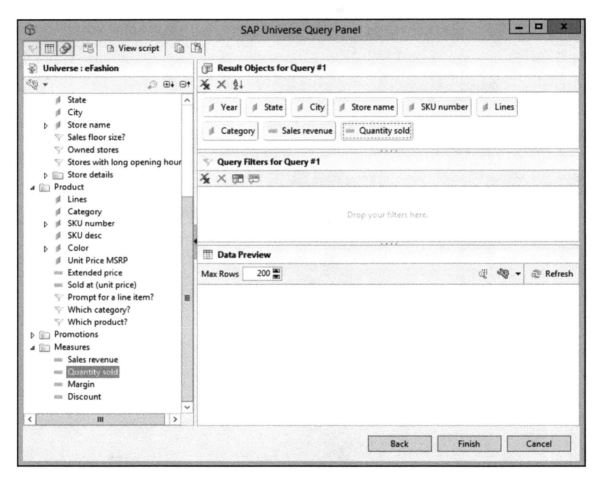

9. Click on **Finish**.
10. Once you have completed all of the preceding steps (the preparation phase), the following screen will appear (visualization).
11. From here, we will create the report by putting `Sales revenue` on **X Axis** and `Category` on **Y Axis**. Choose **Create** from the `MEASURES` screen area and then drag `Sales revenue` onto **X Axis** and `Categogy` onto **Y Axis**, as follows:

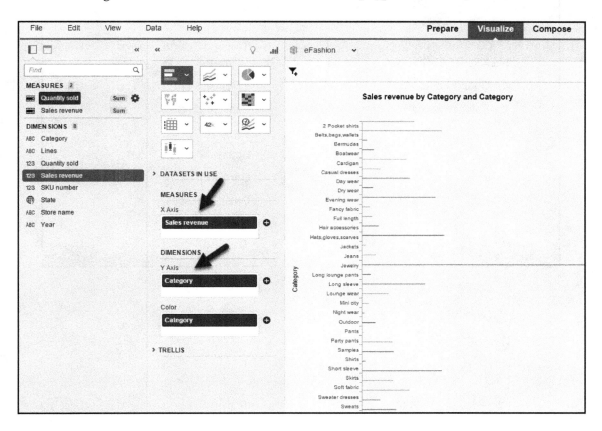

12. Change the orientation to horizontal. Use the **Include** option to filter for the category 2 Pocket shirts. You can do this by clicking the **Horizontal Orientation** button (as pointed to by the arrow in the following diagram). The measures and dimensions will appear across the top:

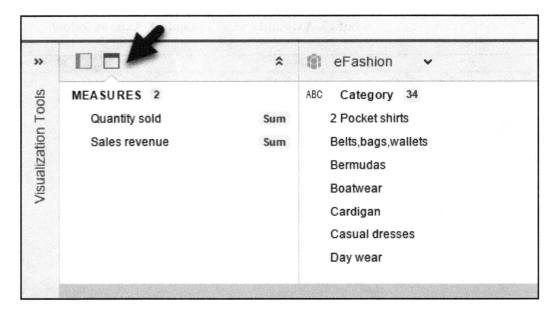

13. Choose **Include** | **2 Pocket DE** | **Enter**:

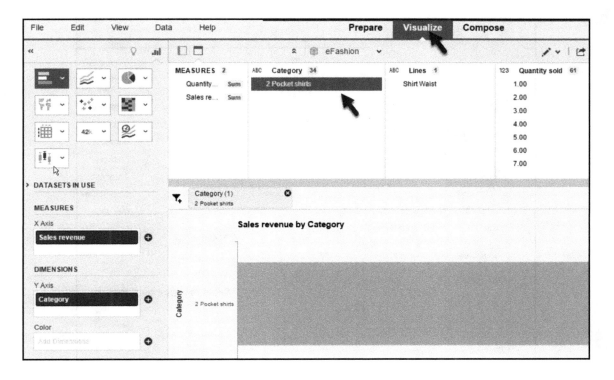

14. Now, we can save it to our local computer, as follows:

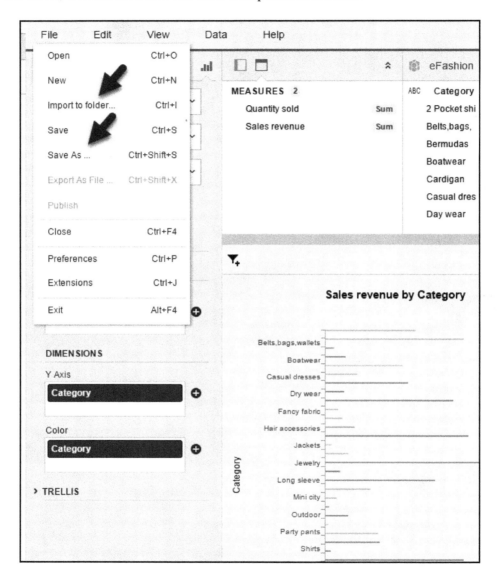

15. We have some new save options for the document (**Local**, **Server for teams**, and **SAP BI Platform**) when we try to save it. Choose the option that best suits your requirements:

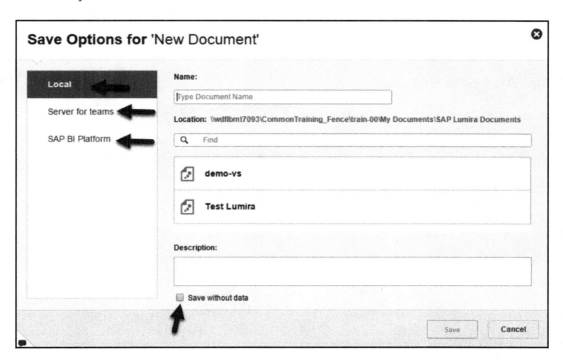

16. As we saw previously, you also have the option to **Save without data**. All of the documents that are created without this check box being checked means that the Lumira documents will contain no data until the time a user explicitly saves them. For instance, if we are modifying such a document on the SAP Lumira Server for BIP and choose **Save**, it would save the document with the data loaded when you opened the document. If you wish to save just your changes and not the data, then you should click on **Save without data**.

17. Now, let's try to create a new report. This time, we will use a hierarchy. The steps for connecting to the `eFashion` dataset remain the same.

18. We add the same dimensions and measures to the results panel, that is, `Year`, `Store name`, `Category`, `Lines`, `SKU number`, `Sales revenue`, and `Quantity sold`:

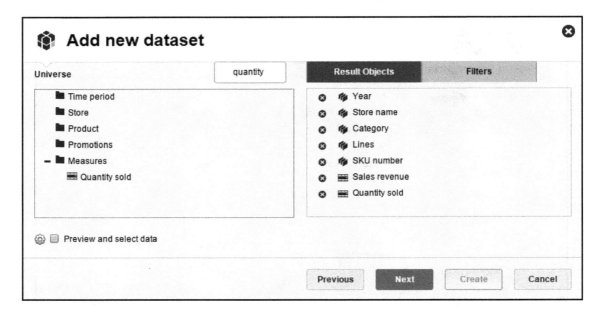

19. Filter the data in the query so that we have optimal performance for the year 2004. Create the report with `Sales revenue` on the **X Axis** and `Category` on the **Y Axis**:

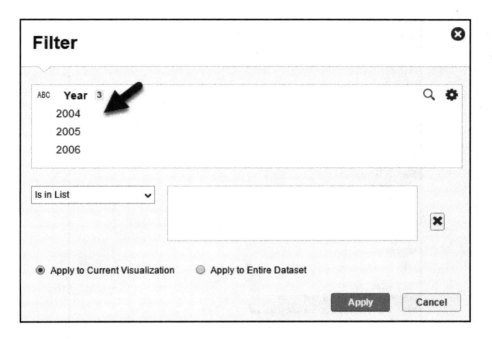

20. Now, we will create a custom hierarchy with Lines, Category, and SKU number as levels. In the dimensions screen area, hover over SKU number and choose the **Options** icon. Choose **Create a custom hierarchy**, as follows:

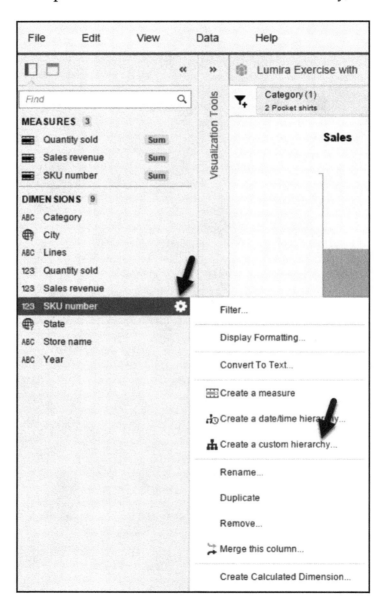

21. In the **Create Hierarchy** dialog box, add `Lines`, `Category`, and `SKU number` in
    that order. Enter a name for the hierarchy named `Hierarchy` and click on
    Create:

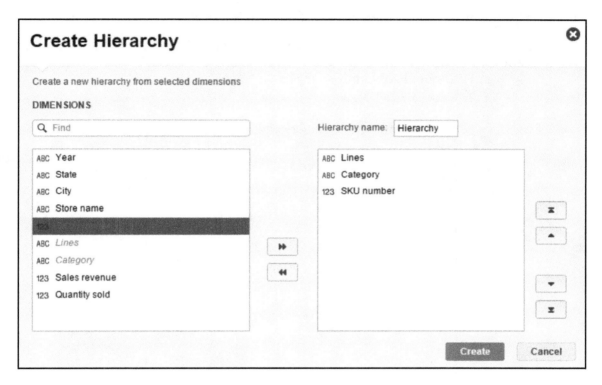

22. Create a pie chart visualization with `SKU_Hierarchy` and `Sales revenue`.
    Alternatively, you can use a different representation to visualize the data. Then,
    save it, like we did earlier.

Creating a visualization using a SAP BW query

Now, we will use SAP BW query to create a visualizaton.

Let's start by creating a SAP Lumira visualization from SAP BW connections (BW query):

1. First, we launch SAP Lumira and create a new report based on the BW data source:
    1. Choose **SAP Lumira** | **Open**
    2. Choose **File** | **New**:

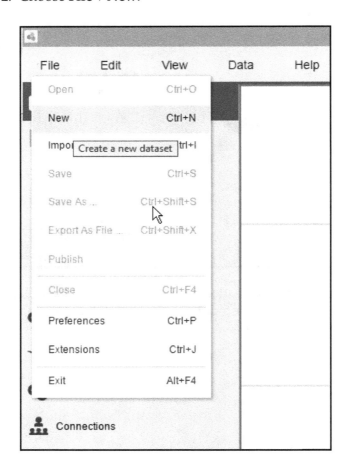

3. In **Add new dataset**, choose **Download from SAP Business warehouse:**

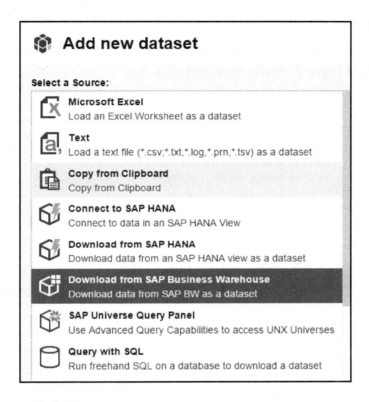

4. Click **Next**

2. In the **SAP BW Data Acquisition Connector** window, change the **connect To** value to **SAP BusinessObjects BI platform**. Enter the credentials that were provided by your administrator. Choose **Connect** and then choose the appropriate data source:

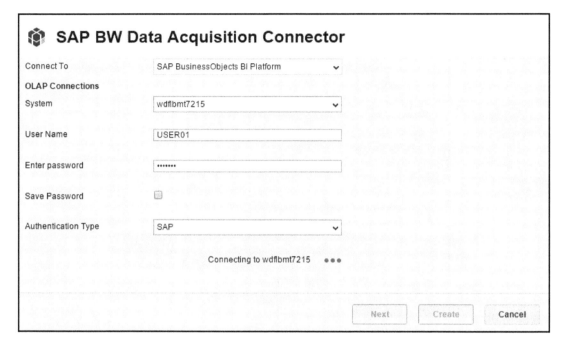

3. Select the query that you want to use for your storyline. In the measure section, select all of the required measures. Choose **Add** to move them to the **create your Lumira Dataset** section. Repeat this step for all the dimensions.
4. Make sure that both the article ID (key) and description (text) will be downloaded to SAP Lumira:
   1. Select the article dimension
   2. Click the gear icon and choose **presentation | Key & Text**
   3. Choose the **Create | Lumira visulaization** screen that appears

5. Now, we will define the report. `Amount sold` should be on the *x* axis and `Category` should be on the *y* axis:
    1. From the `MEASURES` screen area, drag `Amount sold` to the **X Axis**
    2. From the `MEASURES` screen area, drag `Category` to the **Y Axis**

6. We will now change the orientation to horizontal and also include the option to filter for the category:
    1. Choose the **Horizontal Orientation** button. The measures and dimensions will appear across the top.
    2. Use the scroll bar near the top half of the screen to show the dimensions that didn't fit on the screen.
    3. Move your cursor over `Category` and click the **Options** button.
    4. Choose **Include.**
    5. Enter the filter criteria (I chose **DE**) and click on **Enter.**
    6. Click on `Region` and ensure that only `Germany` data is displayed.

7. We will now use the **Options** button to remove the filter for `Category` by cleaning the selection:
    1. Move the pointer over `Category` | **Options**
    2. Choose **Clear Selections**

8. Name the report (I named it `Lumira_demo_sales`) and save the report to your local computer:
    1. Choose **File**| **Save**
    2. Choose **Local**
    3. Enter the **Name** and **description**
    4. Choose **Save**

9. Now, we can also try using the BW hierarchy with the preceding report. We will also explore the filtering and cross-tab presentation:
   1. Step 1 to 3 are the same (until query selection).
   2. Select all of the measures and dimensions on the left-hand side. Make sure to expand the `Category` dimension on the left to show the `Category` hierarchy.
   3. Use the **Add** icons option to move them to the right-hand side (including the `Category` hierarchy).
   4. Expand the `Category` hierarchy levels.
   5. Expand the **+** sign next to the **Category** dimension twice.
   6. Select the `Category` hierarchy that's at the lowest level.
   7. Hover over this object until the **Settings** icon appears and then select it.
   8. In the **Level Selection** dialog box, choose the **User Defined** radio button.
   9. In the **Level Range** field, enter 5 and then click **OK**.

10. We will now make sure that both the article key (article ID) and article text (description) can be downloaded to SAP Lumira:
    1. Select the article dimension and hover over it until you see the gear icon
    2. Choose **Presentation** | **Key & Text**

11. Now, we will build **Crosstab** with **Gross Amount** on the **X Axis** and **Product Text** on the **Y Axis**:
    1. Choose **Create**. The Lumira visualization screen will appear.
    2. Drag `Quantity sold` to the **X Axis**.
    3. Drag `Family` to the **Y Axis**.
    4. Drag `State` to the **Y Axis** under `Family`.
    5. Click the **Crosstab** button.

12. Change to a horizontal orientation and filter the data to show data from `State` of `Califonia`. Then, we will check what happens for available options for `City`:

    1. Choose the **Horizontal Orientation** button, scroll to find the `State` dimension, and select `California`.

    2. Review the available cities in the `City` column.

    3. Now, we can also check for a BW external category hierarchy that we would have previously downloaded to Lumira. Drilling down to the `Category` level of the pie chart, remove all filters. Also, swap `Amount sold` for `Quantity sold`.

    4. Choose the **Vertical Orientation** button.

    5. Remove all of the filters in the visualization by choosing the **Close** button on the dimension in the **Filter** bar.

    6. Drag `Amount sold` directly onto `Quantity sold` in the `MEASURES` panel. Then, drag out `Quantity sold`.

    7. Drag out `City` and `State` from the rows and drag in the hierarchy.

    8. Choose the pie chart icon.

    9. Select the **All Categories** segment (the largest segment).

    10. In the dialog box, choose **Filter** and select the pie chart for the categories that are included in the custom hierarchy when it's created.

    11. Select the pie chart and select drill down from the dialog box. Hover over the pie segments to see the segment on the right represents the categories for men.

    12. Select the pie segment on the right and select drill down from the dialog box. Hover over the pie segments to see which categories they contain and the quantity that's been sold for each one.

    13. Select a segment. Choose drill up from the dialog box.

13. Name the report (I named it `Lumira_demo_sales_Hierarchy`) and save the report to your local computer:

    - Choose **File** | **Save**
    - Choose **Local**
    - Enter the **Name** and **Description**
    - Choose **Save**

Creating a SAP Lumira storyboard

In the previous section, we learned how to create a visualization with various data sources. Now, we can combine these visualization pieces into a storyboard. Let's quickly run through steps of how to create a storyboard:

1. Launch SAP Lumira and go to **Compose**:

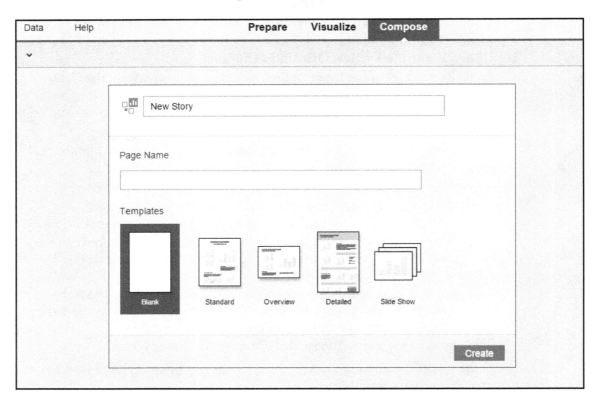

2. Open an existing SAP Lumira sample document so that we can design some contest results. Choose **Try with samples** and double-click it. Here, I will use the same report that we created previously.

3. Open the **Prepare** tab page and determine the source of the data for this document. Choose the **Prepare** tab page. If you are using the sample document, in the top right, you will see that the source is an Excel document called `Results.xlsx`. Since we are using a report that we created ourselves, we will see the following screenshot:

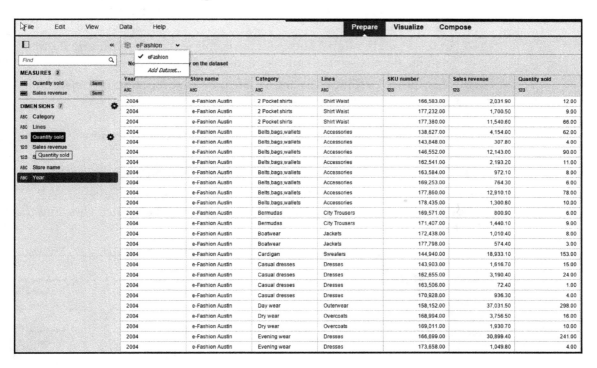

4. To review some of the visualizations that we have, choose the **Visualize** tab and adjust how you want your visualizations to show up in your story (if you are using default data, review the map visualization). The following steps are only required when you use sample data, so they are not relevant for our report:

    1. It is the first one in the list, so it appears when the **Visualize** tab is selected

    2. At the bottom of the tab page, scroll down to find the tag cloud and review the measures and dimensions that it is made up of

    3. Scroll down to select a visualization with just a simple number in it, for example, 289

    4. In the **Visualization Tools** pane, we can see that the **Numeric Point** visualization is selected and only measures are referenced

5. Access the **Compose** tab. Find the name of the only story about this subject and what page the tag cloud visualization is on:

    1. Choose the **Compose** tab.

    2. You can edit and enhance your story with preceding options.

    3. Name your story. It should appear at the top of the page.

    4. Scroll to page 2 to find the tag cloud visualization.

6. Preview the new story storyboard to see how it will appear on a tablet device. You can do this by choosing **Preview** in the **Preview** panel and then choosing the **Tablet Preview** radio button:

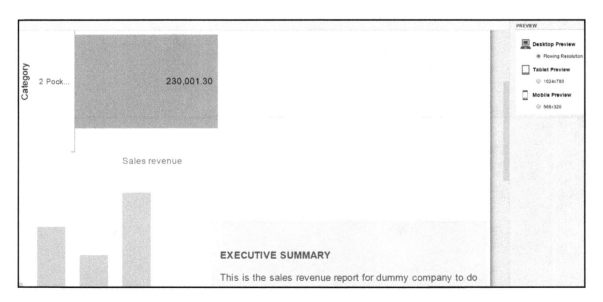

Summary

In this chapter, we got a general overview of SAP Lumira. We learned how to visualize and manipulate data using a SAP Lumira storyboard. We also learned how we can perform data discovery and information delivery with this tool.

In the next chapter, we will learn about SAP Predictive Analytics, where our focus will be more on data mining. We will learn how the SAP Predictive Analytics toolset can be used and we will go into the details of the Automated Analytics and Expert Analytics features of the tool. We will close the chapter by looking at the life cycle of a SAP Predictive Analytics project.

7
SAP BusinessObject Predictive Analytics 2.0

In this chapter, we'll be introduced to SAP BusinessObjects SAP Predictive Analytics and explore the toolsets it has. We'll also learn how the SAP Predictive Analytics toolset can be used and we'll go into the details of the **Automated Analytics** and **Expert Analytics** features of the tool.

In this chapter, we'll cover the following topics:

- Introduction to SAP BusinessObjects Predictive Analytics
- Explore the SAP Predictive Analytics toolsets
- Life cycle of SAP Predictive Analytics project
- Introduction and usage of Automated Analytics
- Expert Analytics and its usage

Introduction to SAP BusinessObjects Predictive Analytics

SAP BusinessObjects Predictive Analytics allows us to create, deploy, and maintain statistical models and data mining solutions, with which we can get insights on our data to make predictions of future events.

It enables users to perform time series forecasting, outlier detection, trend analysis, classification analysis, segmentation analysis, and affinity analysis, to name but a few of the multiple types of analysis it offers. The analysis is coupled with visualization techniques so as to help users create a story with the help of charts and decision trees. In addition, it also offers various analytical algorithms (namely, predictive) as out of the box and supports the use of R open source statistical analysis.

 There are many overlapping terms in the area of SAP Predictive Analytics but our focus will be more on data mining while other tools from SAP BusinessObjects such as SAP Lumira visualization provide insight into historical data. SAP Predictive Analytics forecasts future events.

An algorithm is a procedure or formula for solving a problem while solving specific business problems was the driving force in developing the statistical, data mining, predictive analysis, and machine learning models. Some models were also developed to provide new features and capabilities. We can choose models and methods based on our needs and purposes.

SAP Predictive Analytics delivers many algorithms, many of which were recoded to run on SAP HANA if you have this database. In addition, custom algorithms written in the R language can be executed by SAP Predictive Analytics. In addition to more common algorithms, Automated Analytics has the following:

- Colocation analysis
- Frequent path analysis
- Social network analysis

These algorithms show objects or people in the same location at the same time (colocation analysis), the most common route taken from one a location to another location (frequent path analysis), and who contacts whom (social network analysis), respectively.

We also have the following broader categories of algorithms:

- **Supervised learning**: Is the machine learning task inferring a function from the training data with a target—will the customer buy (yes/no)? In this case, the training data consists of a set of training examples—each example is a pair consisting of an input object (typically, a set of explanatory variables) and a desired output value (the target).

- **Unsupervised learning**: Is the machine learning task finding hidden structures when there's no target? An example is grouping related customers. Some algorithms require training or supervised learning. For example, the model might need to know the profile and demographics of customers that purchased something you were selling and those that didn't. It would then be trained to predict what types of people would most likely buy next time. The first part of this is the so-called **learning phase**.

We can also discuss some of the basic predictive modeling algorithms:

- Classification : classification is the problem of identifying to which of a set of categories (sub-populations) a new observation belongs, on the basis of a training set of data containing observations (or instances) whose category membership is known.
    - Decision tree analysis
    - Neural networks
- Regression
- Clustering or segmentation
- Association rule analysis
- Outlier analysis
- Time series analysis and modeling

SAP Predictive Analytics consists of two distinct toolsets:

- **Automated Analytics**: A wizard-like, easy to use tool that targets all user types (previously, infinite insight)
- **Expert Analytics**: An advanced flexible tool that targets advanced users and data scientists (previously, SAP Predictive Analysis)

SAP Automated Analytics and Expert Analytics features

SAP Automated Analytics provides business analysts and data scientists with a fully automated process that simplifies the setup of the data and the settings for the algorithms without sacrificing statistical validity.

SAP Automated Analytics has the following features:

- Automated data encoding
- Regression/classification
- Segmentation
- Forecasting
- Association rules
- Social network analysis
- Recommendations

SAP data manager allows you to create dynamic datasets that you can move through time. This improves productivity when developing models and applying models in different time frames. This approach is optimized to work with **SAP Model Manager**.

SAP Model Manager is a web server-based thin-client application that allows us to automate modeling activity. Several users can work on the same modeling project with the help of SAP Model Manager by scheduling the following types of tasks:

- Retraining a model
- Applying a model to a new dataset
- Detecting model deviations
- Detecting the deviation of a dataset

One of the limitations of SAP Model Manager is its platform: it's only supported on Microsoft Windows; if our modeling server is deployed on Unix, we would need an additional Windows server.

Both Expert Analytics and Automated Analytics have tight integration to SAP HANA. Analytical Predictive Library comprised of data mining functions from Automated Analytics that were made available within SAP HANA for in-database model development. Automated Analytics algorithms can be executed in SAP's in-memory database HANA. This provides the power to analyze millions of records in seconds.

SAP Lumira visualization enables analysts to visually explore data, produce dashboards, and share this insight with colleagues. With the help of sophisticated algorithms, SAP Expert Analytics helps us to understand and take the next step in the business and modeling outcomes.

SAP Expert Analytics has the following features:

- It performs statistical analysis on our data to understand trends and detect outliers in our business data
- It can access almost any data due to the depth of connectivity
- It allows users to build models and apply to the scenarios so that they can forecast potential future outcomes
- It uses huge data volumes and in-memory processing as it's optimized for SAP HANA
- Expert Analytics is more flexible and has better visualizations but requires more skill and experience to use correctly

R integration is a programming language for data scientists. In SAP Expert Analytics, you can customize algorithms written in R integration. Some of the salient features of R integration with SAP Expert Analysis are as follows:

- Drag and drop and no coding
- Custom R algorithms programming
- Access to over 5,000+ algorithms and packages
- More algorithms and packages than SAS, SPSS, and StatSoft
- A growing number of data analysts in the industry, government, consulting, and academia are now using R
- Embedding R scripts within SAP HANA database execution

The **Predictive Analysis Library** (**PAL**) is designed to provide high performance on big data, and is mainly targeting real-time analytics. It's a built-in C++ library that's designed to perform in-memory data mining and statistical calculations.

Cross-Industry Standard Process for Data Mining (CRISP-DM) was developed in 1996 by Daimler Chrysler, NCR, and ISL. The idea was to map business understanding and data understanding phases. On the flip side, it doesn't the next steps after deployment.Below is the graphical representation of Cross Industry Standard process for Data Mining showing the different phases .

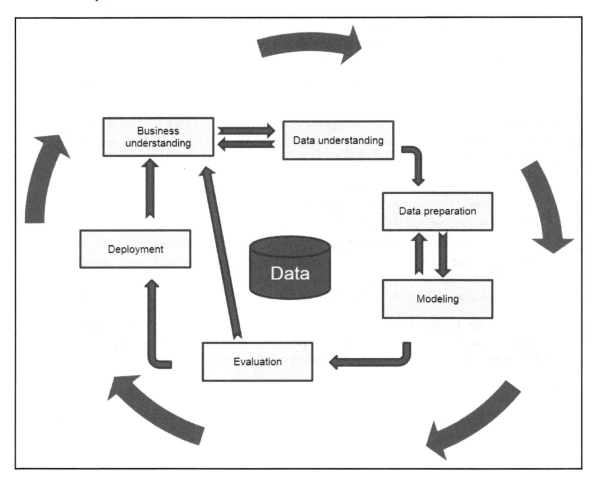

The data understanding phase

This phase includes identifying variables involved in a specific business problem and understanding the values of these variables. The variables in this context are just data fields that are either calculated or provided in data to be analyzed. They aren't the same things as BW variables or prompts.

Most of the time, our data isn't ready to be put into an algorithm without preparation. It should be noted that much of this preparation is automatically performed by SAP Automated Analytics, but not as much is done by the Expert Analytics toolset. With data exploration, we can get summary statistics and visualizations, and this might include various data preparations and transformations. With data transformation, we can create new variables that are to be included in the analysis or to improve the KI of existing variables. Transformations and sampling take place during the preparation phase in a data mining project. Missing values in a dataset can arise from a data supply error or when values/fields simply aren't available. They can be removed from the dataset, estimated, or kept.

The modeling and evaluation phase

Preparation involves splitting datasets with known results into sections for different uses during the modeling and evaluation phase of a project. Central to predictive modeling is a train-and-test regime.

Data is partitioned into training and test subsets. There are a variety of cutting strategies (random, sequential, periodic, and so on). We build our model on the training subset (called the **estimation subset**) and evaluate its performance on the test subset (a hold-out sample called the **validation subset**). The test and train theme has extensions, for example, a random splitting of a sample into training and test subsets could the unexpected and unpredictable, especially when working with small datasets. So we must conduct (on ad hoc) statistical experiments by executing a number of random splits and average performance indices from the resulting test sets.

A classification example using Automated Analytics

Classification identifies the category that a new observation belongs to, on the basis of a training set of data containing observations whose category membership is known. Classification models are used for predicting a binary (one/zero or yes/no) type of response. In our example, we'll build a model of who or who won't respond to a marketing campaign. Our classification model defines the relationships between input variables. In our example, the output, referred to as the dependent variable or target variable, is a field called **class** and a bunch of other demographic profile attributes of the customers are referred to as the independent variables or the explanatory variables. We use known input and output variables to define a model, and then use the model to predict or score unknown values. This is referred to as supervised learning or directed data mining. The classification model provides many output variables for meaningful analysis of the data. A mathematical rule is generated for use in applying the model to new datasets where we don't know the result, and a graphical tree is generated to clearly show what the most important factors in the decision process are.

Model performance indicators

We'll restrict our discussion specifically to SAP, as this is a huge topic and we can't cover all aspects of it. We'll focus on two of the existing and commonly used pieces of statistical data—**Predictive Power (KI)** and **Predictive Confidence (KR)**.

A KI indicator zero (a pure random model) to one (a perfect ideal model) measures the capacity of the input variables (explanatory variables) to explain the target—that is, the proportion of the target's variability that's explained by the model. How good the KI can be completely depends on the business case and available data. We can improve the KI of a model by adding new variables to the training dataset or combining explanatory variables.

On the other hand, when we need to know the robustness of a model, we would have to look for KR. It shows the capacity of the model to get the same performance when it is applied to a new dataset that has the same characteristics as the training dataset. A model with a prediction confidence of *0.98* or greater is considered to be robust while anything less than *0.95* should be reconsidered with precaution. We can increase the KR by adding new observations to the training dataset.

Please keep in mind that, although KI and KR are unique to SAP Automated Analytics and to a lesser degree Expert Analytics, they are in turn based on very sound mathematical footings; they just help to simplify the process of finding an effective model for a given situation.

Expert Analytics builds on the core of the code of SAP Lumira to add extensive and customized execution of data mining algorithms to an already powerful visualization platform. Although they share code under the covers, SAP Predictive Analytics is a much more sophisticated solution and it costs much more to license. Expert Analytics builds the predictive models with data manipulation components that have been organized together in collections of components called an **analysis**. There can be many different analysis for multiple different source datasets in the same document.

The components of Expert Analytics are as follows:

- Data preparation
- Algorithms
- Models to execute after training
- Data writing to store the results set in a database or file

A time series is a set of historical data entries that have been over time that are used to predict values for the future. With a time series model, say, for example, triple exponential smoothing, we can forecast future time periods for a continuous variable. It can include factors such as trend and cyclical patterns (seasonality). The basic output is predictions for future periods and line graphs that visualize these predictions.

To try out some of the preceding concepts, we would need some sample data. You can download this data from the following URL: `https://developers.sap.com/uk/tutorials/mlb-hxe-import-data-pa.html`. The preceding URL tells you step by step how to import SAP Predictive Analytics datasets in 4 steps. These steps could be summarized as follows:

1. Prepare your environment. Since this chapter needs the installation of the Predictive Analytics tool with SAP HANA, a reader who doesn't have SAP HANA can download the trial version and prepare the environment as per the following blog: `https://developers.sap.com/tutorials/mlb-hxe-setup-basic.html`.

2. To create a dedicated schema, go to HANA Studio and execute the SQL query: `CREATE SCHEMA PA_DATA;`.

3. Import methods connected to the **HXE** tenant using `ML_user` (this is from step 1) and execute the following SQL statement:

```
Select * from M_INIFILE_CONTENTS WHERE SECTION =
'import_export' and Key =
'enable_csv_import_path_filter'rt_path_filter'
```

The sample dataset is available and the steps are again mentioned at `https://developers.sap.com/tutorials/mlb-hxe-import-data-sql-import.html`.

- Preparing SAP Predictive Analytics datasets - this step and the following steps of downloading the data and rule can be performed from the link: `https://help.sap.com/viewer/p/SAP_PREDICTIVE_ANALYTICS` (under the *Samples* section-census data):
  - Association rule dataset
  - Census dataset
  - Geo localization dataset
  - Social dataset
  - Text coding dataset
  - Time series dataset

Please follow the URL or blog completely to get all of the datasets in your system: `https://help.sap.com/viewer/p/SAP_PREDICTIVE_ANALYTICS` (under the *Samples* section).

Automated Analytics – forecasting in SAP Predictive Analysis

Now, let's try our hand with what we learned earlier and use the datasets that we've imported into our system. We'll go phase by phase.

Configuring the Modeler and exploring the data

Let's configure **Modeler**:

1. In Windows, search for `predictive Analytics`:

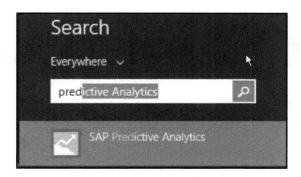

2. Choose the **SAP Predictive Analytics** application and choose **Modeler**:

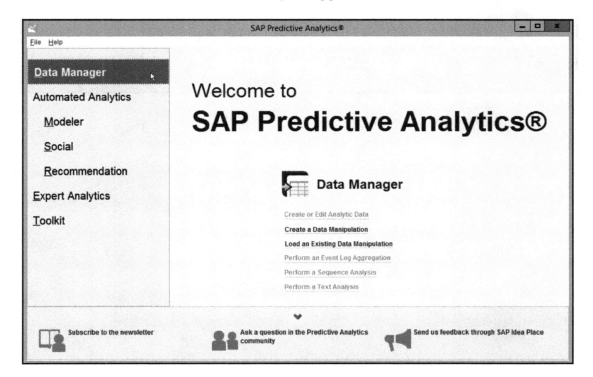

3. Select **Create a Classification/Regression Model**:

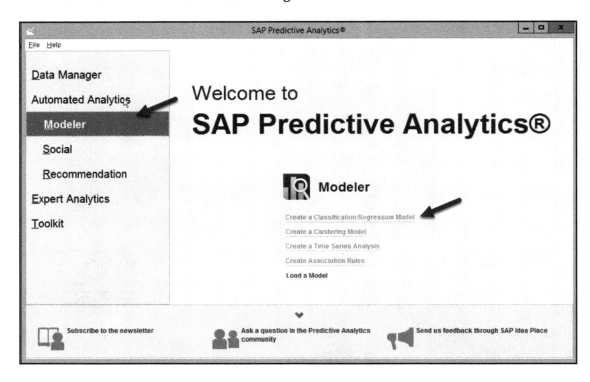

4. Use the `Census01.csv` file that we downloaded previously:

For exploring the data we need to perform following steps:

1. We can explore the data before using it:

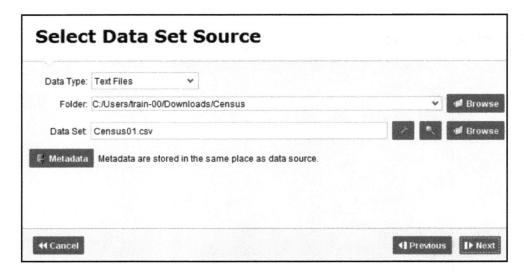

2. Choose the magnifying glass icon and look for values in the `class` column. We will find that the `class` column has values of either 1 or 0 (customers who purchased or customers who didn't purchase):

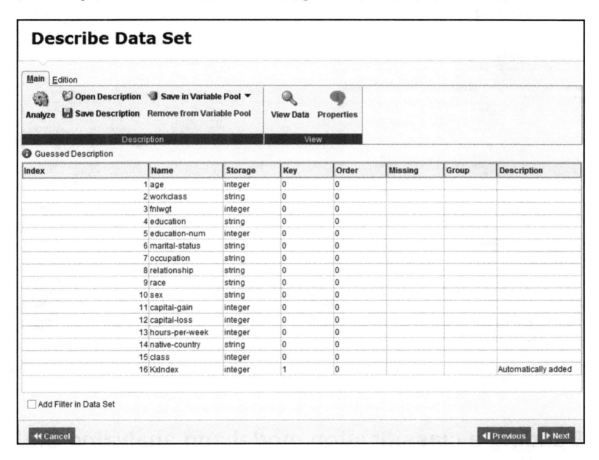

3. We can also explore analyzed category frequencies and find the frequency of the target groups that purchased a particular class:

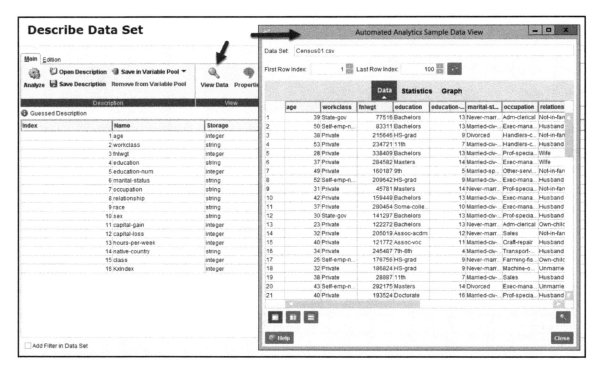

4. Analyze the continuous variables: just play around with various factors and values.

Building a classification model and analyzing the results

Now, we'll build an initial model using the defaulted variable selection and continue to the model summary page.

To build a classification model, perform these steps:

1. Go to the **data subscription** page and choose **Next**.
2. We'll now have the **Variable Selection** page. When you choose **Next,** we'll reach the summary of the modeling parameter page:

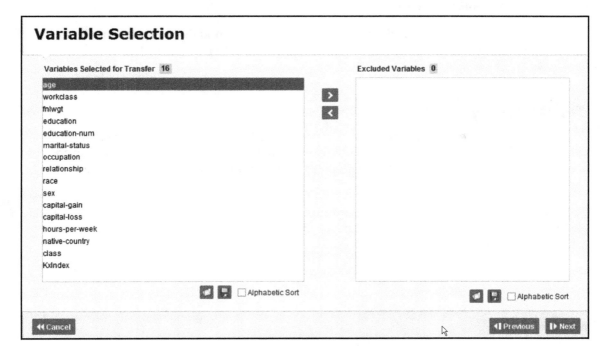

3. Select both the **Compute Decision Tree** and **Enable Auto-Selection** checkboxes and then click **Generate**.
4. We can now review the model summary and determine whether the new data can be added by viewing the KI and KR. The model K1 is *.81* and the KR is *.99*. The KR is over *.95* and that means that the model can be applied to new data with confidence.

To analyze the results, perform the following steps:

1. On the training the model page, click **Next** and select **Model Graphs**. Now, we can see the **Detected Profit**.
2. We can review the results with various section criteria by selecting **contributions by variable**, as an example.

Similarly, we can use the other datasets and build various models to explore and practice our learning. I leave it to the readers to try their hand at different datasets.

Summary

In this chapter, we learned about how to use SAP Predictive Analytics; our focus was more on data mining. We also learned how the SAP Predictive Analytics toolset can be used and we went into details about the Automated Analytics and Expert Analytics features of the tool.

In the next chapter, we'll learn about common reporting features across SAP BI tools. We'll also focus on methods of making reports available on mobile devices, followed by scheduling and emailing SAP BO WebI documents.

Section 3: BI Platform Features and Deployment

3

This section describes the SAP BusinessObjects BI platform features, including reporting, scheduling, and distribution, and shows how to deploy the platform (with a use case). It consists of two chapters: Chapter 8, *BI Platform Features*, which covers the features of the platform. In Chapter 9, *BI Platform Deployment*, we talk in detail about the deployment strategy and factors that should be considered while in deployment. In this section, we learn in detail about the deployment and configuration of SAP BusinessObjects BI platform 4.2.

The following chapters will be covered in this section:

- Chapter 8, *BI Platform Features*
- Chapter 9, *BI Platform Deployment*

BI Platform Features

8

In this chapter, we will discuss common reporting features that can be found across SAP BI tools. We will also learn how reports can be made available on mobile devices, followed by scheduling and emailing SAP BusinessObjects Web Intelligence documents.

In this chapter, we will learn about the following topics:

- BI platform features
- Methods of making reports available on mobile devices
- Scheduling and emailing an SAP BusinessObjects Web Intelligence report

Introduction to the BI platform features of SAP BusinessObjects

Business Intelligence tools are the starting point for SAP BusinessObjects Mobile. With the exception of SAP BusinessObjects analysis for Microsoft Office, the other SAP BusinessObjects BI tools provide good support for mobile deployment. Mobile apps are the future of data consumption and analysis. Integrating your mobile device into your analytical world is just natural progression. iOS and Android are supported, and there is also limited support for BlackBerry. Specific mobile platforms support different SAP BI tools. We will look at this in more detail later. For specific versions supported by each OS, refer to the Mobile PAM.

SAP BusinessObjects Mobile is the only app you need for high-quality reporting. Mobile reporting provides the following benefits:

- Access to your business data anywhere, anytime
- Connections to live business data and make smarter decisions
- An interactive experience for business users and executives

- The ability to intuitively access, navigate, and analyze data
- Smart search for relevant information
- SAP BusinessObjects Mobile architecture

The following diagram illustrates the architecture of the SAP BusinessObjects Business Intelligence platform 4.2:

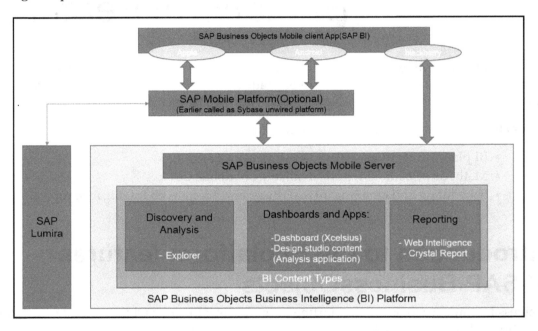

The preceding diagram defines the following BI tool grouping: discovery and analysis; dashboarding and apps; and reporting. These groupings are important because different groupings are supported by different operating systems for mobile devices (except for iOS, no other OS supports all of these groupings).

The SAP BusinessObjects Mobile solution enables a user to make faster and informed decisions on the fly based on the visualization that was created based on SAP BusinessObjects Intelligence's content and data. It contains three components:

- SAP BusinessObjects Mobile client (SAP BI app)
- SAP BusinessObjects Mobile server
- SAP BusinessObjects Business Intelligence platform server

These also have optional elements for enhanced security in the landscape:

- A reverse proxy server
- A sybase unwired platform server with a relay server

SAP BusinessObjects BI platform security

Let's take a quick look at the security aspect of the platform and learn how to administer security. We will start our discussion with user and group setup. The user and group management area enables us to access (role, permission, access) and work on the SAP **BusinessObjects Business Intelligence (BOBI)** platform. By default, there are three user accounts in the BOBI platform:

Account	Description
Administrator	This is the most powerful default user account that comes with the BOBI platform. With this account, a user can perform administrative duties in the BI platform application (such as the central management console, publishing wizard, and BI launch pad). This account belongs to the administrator and everyone group.
Guest	This account belongs to the everyone group by default. It is disabled (by default) and is not assigned a password by the system. In the case where we assign a password to the guest account, the single sign-on to the BI launch pad will break and will no longer work.
SMAdmin	SAP solution manager uses this account, which has read-only privileges. With it, it can access BI platform components. It is mainly used for system monitoring and other system administrative tasks from the solution manager system.

License type and access

The BI platform supports four types of licenses given here:

- **Concurrent user**: The license for concurrent users are usage based, concurrently (simultaneously) regarding how many users can connect at a given time to the BI platform. These are mainly used by occasional users who require access as per their needs.
- **Named user**: These are the users (mainly) who get (require) access to the BI platform, irrespective of the number of concurrent users who are logged in.

- **BI analyst**: This license gives the user the authority to access, edit, create, and design reports. It is possible for the user to perform administrative tasks in the central management console. This license should be provided to users who are mainly creating content in the BI platform.
- **BI viewer**: These users are not allowed to access the CMC. It is for users who are primarily consumers of BI platform content. This content cannot be modified and is only used for report viewing, unlike BI analyst.
- **User settings**: The group concept is very handy, especially for the mass modification/creation of users (role and privileges). Just like with groups, we can modify/change at one place rather than doing it individually for each user. The same applies for assigning object rights to a group or groups, which can again be done in one go.

User rights and permissions

When a user account is created, it is possible to modify its properties, which are as follows:

- **Account name**: This is a unique name that's given to identify a user's account. This is the username that a user will have to use to log in to the intelligence platform.
- **Full name**: This contains a specific user's entire name. This is an optional field, but it is recommended that it is used as it proves useful when you are managing multiple users.
- **Email**: This field contains the email address of a user and is completely optional. It is used for reference purposes only. This proves useful in case you have forgotten your password – the administrator is then able to retrieve the email address from this given field and send the password of the user's account to the respective user.
- **Description**: This field is used to add information about the user, such as their position, department, or location (geographical). This field is optional.
- **Connection type**: This option specifies how the user connects to the SAP BusinessObjects Business Intelligence platform based on their license agreement.
- **Enterprise password setting**: This field grants you privileges of changing your password and the other password settings. This can also be configured in the authentication area of the CMC.
- **Assign alias**: This feature can be used to link accounts for users that have many accounts within SAP BusinessObjects. This results in the user having multiple SAP BOBI platform login credentials that link to one SAP BOBI platform account.

- **Account is disabled**: This field (or rather, checkbox) gives the administrator the privilege of deactivating an account for a particular user, instead of the account getting permanently deleted. This proves highly useful when a user would not be requiring any access to the system temporarily. To activate the account, the checkbox can simply be ticked again.

Group hierarchy, groups, and subgroups

Group hierarchy is for users who share the same account privileges. They can be collectively put into a group. Groups are created based on role, departments, work locations, and so on. With groups in place, access rights and access privileges maintenance becomes very simple and efficient. With groups, we can only modify the groups, and the impact affects all users who are part of the group. Providing access to reports or folders also becomes simpler with the group concept. The following is a list of default groups that are already created by default:

Account	Description
Administrators	This is the group in which users can perform all tasks in all the BI platform applications. Tasks may include publishing, CMC, CCM, and BI launch pad.
Everyone	This is a default group that's automatically given to each user of the platform.
QaaWS group designer	To access query as web service, only those users who are assigned to this group can access it.
Report conversion tool users	For the users who belong to this group, they have access to the reporting tools.
Translators	For any user who has access to this specific group, they will be able to access the translation manager applications.
Universe designer users	The users who belong to this group are entitled to access this application. No users belong to this group by default. The users of this group have access to its respective folders.

The group hierarchy is as follows:

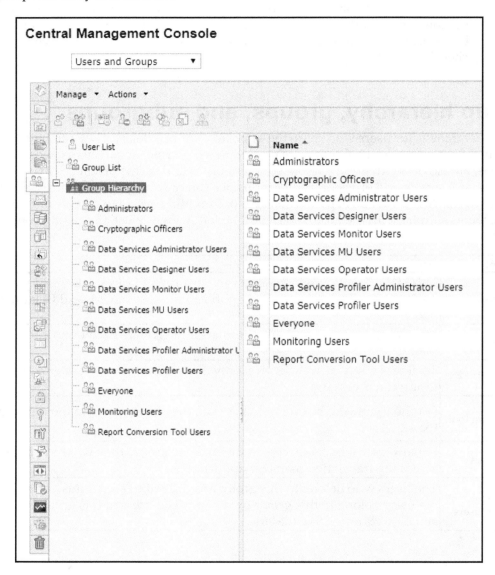

Groups and subgroups: After creating a new group, we can add users, add subgroups, or specify group membership, so that the new group is actually a subgroup. It is useful to create subgroups when we must classify groups of users further. For example, users can be grouped by location (such as Frankfurt), and then further divided according to their department (sales, marketing, and so on).

Rights in the BI platform

One of the major aspects of SAP's BOBI 4.2 implementation is managing security and rights. Data can be secured at the folder level, report level, universe level, and database source level. Security is available in the form of authentication, report, application, data and inheritance. Concepts of rights are used as base units for controlling a user's access to the objects, users, application, servers, and other capabilities of the BI platform. With concepts of rights, we cannot only enable access control to our BI platform, but also delegate user and group management to different departments. Rights are either granted, denied, or not specified to a user or group. Not specified implicitly means that a right is denied. In an ambiguous status, where the access control settings result in a right being both granted and denied, the denied result prevails. The following is a simple cheat sheet for the same (**Denied > Grant > Not Specified**):

```
Grant + Not specified --> Grant

Grant + Denied --> Denied

Grant + Denied + Not Specified --> Denied

Denied + Not Specified --> Denied
```

Let's walk through some of the common terms related to rights so that we have a better understanding of them.

Object-level security

Inheritance is followed in BI platform security, since the objects inherit their security from the parent folder. Until and unless rights are explicitly set at the object level, inheritance prevails. Otherwise, object-level rights override the inherited rights.

Folder-level security

Inheritance is also applicable at the folder level. With folder-level security, we can set access level rights for a folder and the objects contained therein. The approach is top-down here, so the security gets inherited from the parent folder to the subfolders. This is similar to object-level security.

Top-level folder security

The top-down approach is followed here as well, so the root folder passes the right to subobjects. The allocation of access and privileges becomes much easier because, if it has any access levels in common with certain objects types, then we can apply them throughout the whole system and set them at the **Top-Level Security** folder that's specific to each object.

The following screenshot illustrates the CMC, which contains access to top-level security:

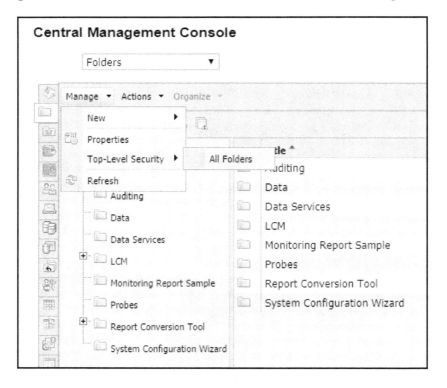

Access levels

Having many rights in the system and assigning individual rights always leads to high maintenance and is not reproducible. With the help of access levels, that is, the collection of rights, we can do the following:

- Assign rights to groups, not individual users
- Build up from minimum rights and increment
- Minimize explicit denies (*Grant + Deny = Deny*)

The BI platform has several predefined access levels. These predefined access levels are based on a model of increasing rights, starting with view and ending with full control. Each access level builds on the rights granted by the previous level.

The following screenshot illustrates the CMC, which contains access levels:

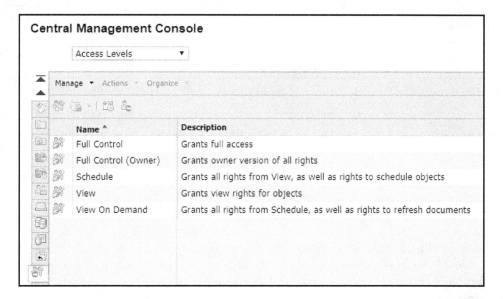

Inheritance

There are two types of inheritance: group inheritance and folder inheritance. Group inheritance gives users the right to inherit rights as the result of group membership. For example, if you create a user called demo user, and add it to an existing group called sales, then demo user will automatically inherit the appropriate rights for each of the reports and folders that the sales group has been added to.

To have full control over object security, CMC allows us to set up advance rights. These advanced rights provide increased flexibility as we can define security levels for objects at a granular level. Some of the available options are as follows:

Rights option	Description
Granted	When the granted option is chosen, the right is granted to a principal.
Denied	When the denied option is chosen, the right is denied to a principal.
Not specified	The right is unspecified for a principal. By default, rights set to not specified are denied.
Apply to object	These are object-level rights. They only become available when we choose either granted or denied.
Apply to sub objects	These are subobject level rights. They only becomes available when we choose either granted or denied.

We will not delve any deeper, as security in itself is a huge topic and is beyond the scope of this book.

Document settings for mobile access

The first technical step in deploying a mobile environment is to deploy the BI Server in your landscape. Please refer to the product availability matrix for details (`http://help.sap.com/bobip`). Special mobile property settings are needed to control the accessibility to the BI inbox on our mobile device. The settings here are related to documents that are sent to the BI inbox only. Access to documents in folders in the BI launch pad are controlled with additional category settings. The look or behavior of the report on mobile devices is controlled by the categories. In addition to this, the mobile category allows access to the reports via the BI Mobile Platform. This is to allow us to control access to sensitive reports in a mobile environment over and above normal access to the folder in the BI launch pad.

The mobile category can be one of the following categories:

- **Personal category:** Visible to only one specific user
- **Corporate category:** Visible to all mobile users in the company

To control what content is visible on the mobile device, we need to follow these steps:

1. Mark the mobile category (mandatory)
2. Add an additional category (optional):
   - **Confidential**: Choose this for documents that must not be stored on the device
   - **Mobile designed**: Choose this for web documents that must follow a specific layout

Web intelligence-specific settings for SAP BusinessObjects mobile and designing studio-specific settings

Web intelligence-specific settings for SAP BusinessObjects mobile: SAP BusinessObjects mobile offers two options for web intelligence-specific settings. These options are triggered based on the assignment of different categories of the web intelligence document. Many of the BusinessObjects Suite tools have specific properties and settings that are associated with rendering on mobile devices.

Design studio-specific settings: Some of the applications that are developed on design studio can be deployed on tablets, phones, or on the desktop. Keeping this in mind, our approach toward designing analytical applications in SAP design studio must be more open and broader. In general, we should avoid enabling complex applications so that they are visible on mobile devices and only allow those simpler applications with summarized data to be deployed to a mobile workforce.

When we are designing design studio applications, we should work with radio button SAPUI5m as the design elements are accessible to the designer and are better optimized for mobile. Initially, m in SAPUI5m meant mobile, but now m means main. Therefore, when we choose SAPUI5 m, it means that we will get application components with a Fiori look and feel. We can find more resources regarding this at `http://scn.sap.com/community/mobile/businessobjects`.

Scheduling and emailing an SAP BusinessObjects Web Intelligence Report

Now, let's try to understand how to schedule and email an SAP BusinessObjects Web Intelligence report. We have the following recurrence patterns available, which we can use to schedule an object:

Pattern	Description
Now	This pattern allows us to run the object immediately. We can click on schedule and the object will run.
Once	This pattern allows us to run the object only once, irrespective of the schedule (it's used immediately or when a specific date/event is triggered).
Hourly	This pattern allows us to run the objects every hour. We will need to specify at what time it should start and end.
Daily	The daily pattern allows us to run the object every day. We can run it once or several times a day. We need to specify at what time it starts and ends.
Weekly	The weekly pattern allows us to run the object every week. We can run it once or several times a week. We will need to specify what time it should start and end.
Monthly	The monthly pattern allows us to run the object every month (once or several times). We need to specify the start and end dates and times.
N^{th} day of month	This pattern selection allows us to run the object on the Nth (selected) day of every month. We are required to give the start and end dates.
First Monday of the month	This pattern selection allows us to run the object on the first Monday of every month. We are required to give the start and end dates.
Last day of month	With this pattern selection, we can run the object on the last day of every month. We are required to give the start and end dates.
X day of the Nth week of the month	This pattern selection allows us to run the object on a particular day of a particular week every month. We need to specify the day and week, as well as the start and end date.
Calendar	With this pattern selection, the object is run as per the predefined (specified dates) factory calendar.

The preceding pattern is supported by the following run option for recurrence:

Run option	Description
Start date/time lists and calendar box	This option works for all patterns except Now and Calender. We need to select the time (hours, minutes, and AM/PM) and the date on which to start running the object. The BI platform runs the object according to the specified schedule, as soon as it can after the start time has passed.
End date/time lists and calendar box	This option works for all patterns except Now and Calender. We need to select the time (hours, minutes, and AM/PM) and the date on which to stop running the object. The BI platform no longer runs an object after the end time has passed.
Hours (N) list and *Minute (X)* list	These options appear when we select the hourly pattern. We need to select the interval (hours and minutes) at which we want to run the object. If we do not enter a value for N or X, the BI platform runs the report every hour.
Days (N) box	This works for the daily pattern.
Checkbox for days (Monday, Tuesday, ..., Friday)	This option appears when we select the weekly pattern. We just need to select the checkbox for days on which we want to run the job.
Months(N) list	This option is for the monthly pattern. We can either fill intervals (in months) at which we want to run, or we can leave it as is.
Day (N) box	This option is for the Nth day of the month pattern. We need to select the day of the month when we want to run it; if no days are selected, the report will run every day.
Week (N) list and *Day (X)* list	This option is for the Xth day of the Nth week of the month pattern. We need to select the day of the month when we want to run it; if no days are selected, the report will run every day.

With the SAP BusinessObject BI platform, we can configure an object or instance for output to a destination other than the default output, that is, the **File Repository Server** (**FRS**). By default, the output instance is stored on the output FRS. With the option of choosing an additional destination, we get the flexibility of delivering instances across our system or to a destination outside our BI platform. The destinations supported are BI inbox; email; FTP server; and filesystem, that is, SAP StreamWork and the default enterprise location. The destination setting for an object or instance can be changed from CMC or the BI launch pad. If the destination setting changes are implemented via CMC, these settings are reflected in the default scheduling settings for the BI launch Pad.

The following are the some of the common formats that are available for scheduled objects:

Format	Description
PDF	.pdf format.
XML	.xml format.
Comma Seperated Value (CSV)	The CSV format places a specified character between values. For this format, we must specify some formatting properties for the report.
Tab Seperated Text (TTX)	Like the CSV format, the TTX format also places a tab character between values. For this format, we must specify some formatting properties for the report.
Rich Text Format (RTF)	This is only seen in a web viewer. It maintains and keep as much formatting as possible, which also consists of graphics.
Crystal reports	This format (.rpt) produces a normal editable report and preserves all output format options.
Crystal reports (read-only)	This format (.rptr) produces a read-only crystal report.
Microsoft Word (97-2003)	When we use this format (.doc), it maintains and keeps the formatting, which also includes graphics.
Microsoft Excel (97-2003)	When we are using this format, it tries to keep the look and feel of the original report. It does not merge the cells and preserves data. For this format, we should specify the format properties of the report.
Microsoft Excel (97-2003) data only	When we use this format, only the data is saved, with each cell representing a field.

Scheduling and sending a Webi document

Let's look at how we can schedule and send a web intelligence document:

1. We need to log into the SAP BusinessObject BI launch pad by going to the **Windows** | **SAP BusinessObject BI** launch pad. Then, we need to enter our username and password and choose **Log On**.
2. Choose the **Document** tab, then **Folders** | **Public Folder**, and then choose the **Web Intelligence report** that you want to schedule.
3. Right-click on the report (say, Sample report) and select **Schedule**.
4. In the **Formats** tab, select **Adobe Acrobat** .
5. In the **destination** tab, select **BI Inbox**.

6. In the **Instance Title** tab, enter the report name (`Sample report`).

7. Click the **Schedule** button; a new instance will be defined. Give it a name, for example, `Demo_Sample` report.

8. Reopen the instance and go to **History - Demo_sample report window**. Right-click our instance of the document and choose **Reschedule**.

9. Choose the **Recurrence** tab and review the options. Then, select **Now** and choose **Run**.

10. Now, we need to set the format to web intelligence by selecting **Format link** and clicking the **Web Intelligence** checkbox.

11. We should review the options without changing anything for caching, events, and the scheduling server.

12. Choose the **Destination** tab and choose **BI Inbox** from the destination options. In the **Find title** field, enter your username and choose **Search** icon. Then, in the result list, select our user.

13. Name the resulting document (I named it `DEMO_SChedule_Sample`). In the **Add Placeholder** field, select **Date Time**.

14. Now, we can execute and schedule our Webi document by choosing **Schedule** and on the next screen choosing **Refresh** until the status changes to success.

15. We can now review our inbox and view the documents by choosing **Home** and clicking on the documents to open them.

Summary

In this chapter, we got a general overview of how to make reports available on mobile devices, followed by scheduling and emailing SAP BusinessObjects Web Intelligence documents.

In the next chapter, we will learn about the SAP BOBI platform architecture, BI systems, and the elements that are contained within BI systems. We will also describe the deployment strategy and the various factors that should be considered while in deployment.

BI Platform Deployment 9

This chapter describes the BI platform architecture and the systems and servers involved in it. We will identify the requirements and then, based on our findings, plan a deployment. Later in this chapter, we will also see some deployment and configuration options and steps for SAP BusinessObjects 4.2. We will look to understand proper deployment strategy and the factors that we should consider during deployment.

In this chapter, we will learn about the following:

- BI platform architecture and system
- Identifying requirements and planning deployment
- Deployment and configuration of SAP BI 4.2
- Deployment administration

Introduction to BI platform architecture

SAP BusinessObjects BI solutions support all of the interaction and analysis needs of the different business users in an organization. With SAP BusinessObjects BI, SAP promises to enable organizations to take advantage of decades of know-how, industry-leading expertise, and BI best practices developed through close collaboration and co-innovation with its partners and customers:

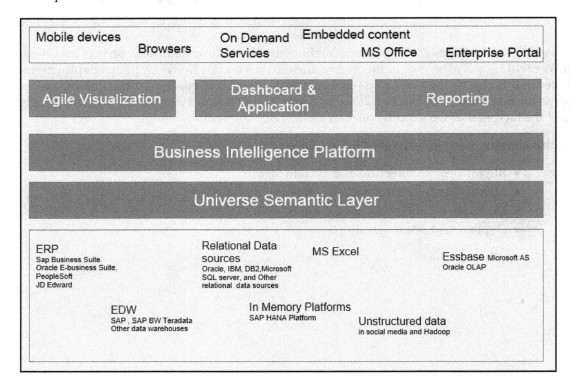

SAP cloud strategy – BI solutions

SAP has been very vocal about being a cloud-focused company. In the endeavor of being a cloud-focused company, SAP has been trying to make all its products available on the cloud, as well as launching cloud-specific solutions. The following are some of the main cloud solutions for BI from SAP.

SAP Analytics Cloud

SAP Analytics Cloud is a **software-as-a-service** (**SaaS**) offering from SAP that facilitates centralized intelligence, automatic insights, and integrated planning and allows interactive results, all in one cloud offering. A customer will have one cloud that provides the ability to give actionable insights to everyone in the organization. Some of the salient features are listed here:

- It supports collaborative planning for an enterprise
- It provides an easy cloud deployment for analytics
- It enables you to perform predictive analytics, and offers machine learning capabilities

SAP Lumira

SAP Lumira is a self-service data manipulation, visualization, and story creation tool that can connect to one or more data sources to create datasets. Lumira has a wide range of graphical charts and tables that enable end users to visualize their data in a more interactive fashion. Users can create stories that provide a graphical narrative to describe this data by grouping charts together on boards to create presentation-style dashboards. Some of the salient features are listed here:

- It provides easy cloud deployment for analytics
- It has a very simple design canvas that encourages the development of collaboration between the business and the IT team
- It includes self-service analytics
- It displays real-time performance and shows insights

SAP BW/4HANA

SAP BW/4HANA combines the capability of SAP BI with the SAP HANA database. Some of the main features of BW/4HANA are as follows:

- It provides cloud and on-premises deployment
- It provides simplified modeling and administration
- It supports effortless integration with SAP and non-SAP applications
- It provides an engaging user experience

SAP Crystal Reports

You can create formatted and dynamic reports from data sources in various formats and in different languages using SAP Crystal Reports. We can turn any data source into interactive, actionable information that can be accessed online or offline from portals and from mobile devices or applications. Some of the salient features are as follows:

- It is an extremely useful and powerful reporting tool that delivers insights in various formats
- It has cloud or on-premises deployment capabilities
- It offers connectivity with diverse data sources
- You can access information online or offline

SAP BusinessObjects BI4 for cloud deployment options

We have the following options available for the deployment of SAP BusinessObjects BI4 to the cloud:

- **SAP hosting partners**: An SAP hosting partner is a third-party hosting partner that already has SAP BI4 experience. Having a hosting partner enables customers to run faster, simpler, and smarter.
- **SAP HANA Enterprise Cloud**: This is a cloud managed by SAP for the SAP HANA, BW on HANA, SUITE on HANA, and SAP BI4 environments.
- **Amazon Web Services**: Customers can deploy SAP BI4 on Amazon's public cloud infrastructure for productive and non-productive purposes without the upfront infrastructure cost.

SAP BusinessObjects on SAP HANA

Having SAP BI on SAP HANA combines the capabilities of **online analytical processing** (**OLAP**) and **Online Transaction Processing** (**OLTP**). The following are the data models that can be used with SAP HANA:

- **Analytic models**:
    - A star schema with a central fact table is used for data foundation
    - Output is typically a calculation view
    - Dimensional and flattened reporting is possible
- **Classical models**:
    - Several tables containing facts
    - JOINS are more complex
    - Reporting is similar to any other **Relational Database Management System** (**RDBMS**)

In the following diagram, we can see how different tools (such as **Lumira** and **Design Studio**) can directly access the information models from an **SAP HANA Database**:

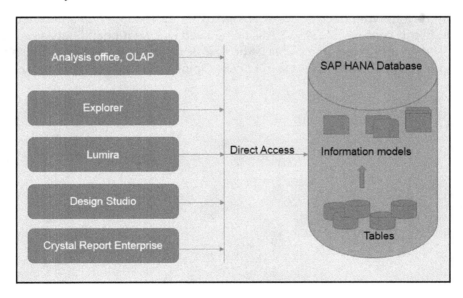

that it should be transparent to the final user of the tools:

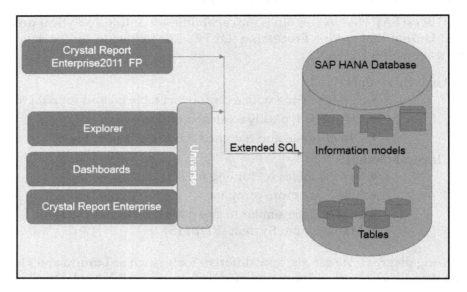

As shown in the following diagram, SAP HANA Analytics is based on a two-tier architecture. In this context, SAP HANA is being used as a relational database system, application server, and web server. This is the first tier. UI clients, which establish the second tier, connect to SAP HANA via HTTP(S), **Open Data Protocol (OData)**, or **SQL/MDX**:

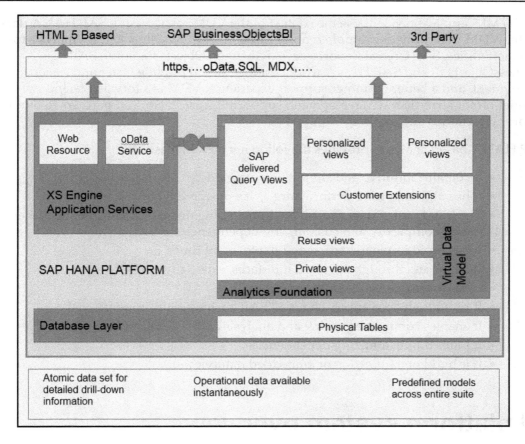

SAP HANA Analytics comprises the following components (initial shipment):

- HTML5-based UIs
- **Virtual Data Model (VDM)** in the form of database views

The HTML5 applications will use the context of the VDM for accessing SAP HANA data. For the VDM, SAP provides sample reports based on SAP BusinessObjects Analysis for Microsoft Office, SAP Crystal Reports, or SAP BusinessObjects Explorer. SAP BusinessObjects BI and SAP HANA work best together to provide faster and easier deployment, and a better customer support experience. VDM is a forward-facing foundation for analytic SAP development, supporting customers, and partners to build reporting scenarios and applications upon it.

SAP HANA-based analytics provides the following advantages:

- It contains intuitive and simplified data models
- It has high reporting performance as it's powered by SAP HANA
- The VDM makes data available without going deeper into SAP models, thereby hiding complexity and customizing dependencies
- It has rapid implementation and deployment times
- It has access through standard interfaces, especially via SQL
- It has more open access with any client
- It provides a once approach for all SAP business suite applications
- It enables common reporting and analysis across applications
- It hides the customizing dependencies.
- It is build on replication or embedded data(views).

BI platform system overview

In general, customers have three core sets of BI requirements: agile visualization, dashboards and applications, and reporting. Keeping this in mind, SAP has designed products that meet customers needs. SAP have products for the following:

- **Discovery, prediction, and creation**: With SAP products, we can do the following:
  - Represent customer stories with visualization
  - Model and adopt data to business needs
  - Discover and optimize the areas of a business that can be optimized

- **Engaging experiences**: With SAP products, we can do the following:
  - Keep track of KPIs and summary data
  - Build customer experience to facilitate quick turnaround times for customers
  - Deliver engaging information on demand
- **Information distribution**: With SAP products, we can do the following:
  - Easily and securely propagate information across an organization
  - Use predefined reports to help find answers to questions
  - Create and print reports for operational work purposes
- **Solutions**: SAP covers the following solutions:
  - **Discovery**: Discovery focuses on analysts and users within the business. The idea of this solution category is to allow users to acquire, clean, and visualize data with minimal end user training. These interfaces have limited capabilities but include powerful features for exploration and navigation. The solutions in this category are created with in-memory data sources in mind, that is, data sources such as SAP HANA. With this approach, we can traverse through data at any level.
  - **Analysis**: SAP's analysis solution focuses mainly on workflows with some additional layouts. Solutions in this category are designed from the ground up as OLAP clients and are well suited for projects with demanding hierarchical navigation requirements. These solutions are built in a way to utilize the benefits of modeled multi-dimensional sources (SAP HANA and **SAP Business Warehouse** (**SAP BW**)) and data in Microsoft SQL Server Analysis Services.
  - **Dashboards**: Dashboards are focused on the needs of the IT and developer community, helping members of the community create and deploy interactive, visual dashboards. These are typically built for end consumers who need tools that provide high visual layouts.
  - **Reporting**: Reporting solutions focus on the mass distribution of formatted data. While SAP Crystal Reports uses a desktop-based report designer, SAP Web Intelligence Designer uses the web. Scheduling and on-demand reporting is possible in both solutions.
  - **Predictive**: The solutions in this category include SAP BusinessObjects Predictive Analytics (we discussed the topic in detail in the previous chapter 7).

SAP BusinessObjects 4.2 – deployment

The following diagram illustrates a highly available SAP BusinessObjects 4.2 deployment with system/auditing databases and the storage tier as a network share. Let's have an overview of a multi-server deployment :

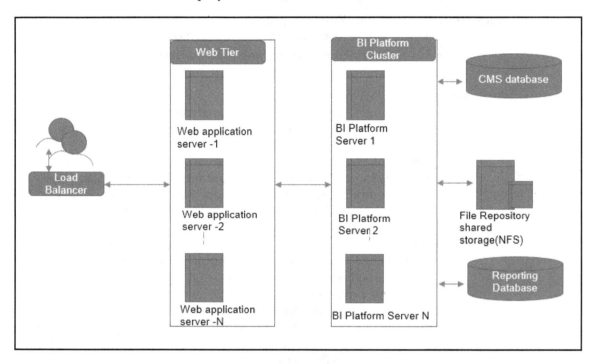

Now, let's discuss the key considerations for some of the components in the preceding diagram in detail.

Central Management Server database requests and system and API calls

We should keep the following things in mind when discussing requests:

- Such calls will be many in number and frequent in nature.
- One HTTP request (such as logon, open report, or refresh report) can generate multiple system and API calls.
- These calls are very short in duration (usually in milliseconds). However, the exception to this is a request to retrieve documents from the File Repository Server, which is more bandwidth-bound than latency-bound.

Centralized versus decentralized

SAP recommends that we should not decentralize **Central Management Server** (**CMS**) services or application servers because of the following reasons:

- CMS services ping other CMSes and BI platform services continuously.
- The network would be impacted more by multiple and frequent requests than an HTTP(S) request over distance.
- We might obtain a slight, barely noticeable gain on web requests, but it would be insignificant compared to the costs incurred.
- Decentralizing will slow the entire system down for every user.

However, decentralization of processing servers could make sense in certain deployment scenarios.

Agile Visualization functions and components

The following are functions and components of Agile Visualization. The Agile Visualization portfolio comprises the following products:

- SAP BusinessObjects Lumira
- SAP BusinessObjects Explorer
- SAP BusinessObjects Analysis
- SAP BusinessObjects Predictive Analytics

With Agile Visualization, we can perform the following activities:

- We can get used to a business environment by bringing together, changing, and enhancing the quality of data
- We can find out trends, outliers, and places of interest in our organization
- We can predict future outcomes based on the current reports

The following are some of the benefits for business analysts and business users:

- Using SAP BusinessObjects Lumira, people can immediately massage, transform, and personalize data without scripting
- With SAP BusinessObjects Explorer, people can immediately search to receive fast answers
- Customers can access tools everywhere using mobile, web-based, and desktop access, whether online or offline
- Customers receive the best SAP BW support with analysis

SAP BusinessObjects Lumira

SAP BusinessObjects Lumira helps us to learn about our organization's data, personalize it according to our liking, and ultimately results in amazing content. Some of the key features are listed here:

- It can be quickly downloaded and installed on a desktop
- It supports business scenarios where data needs to be brought together, transformed, and enhanced
- It can provide insights from many data sources
- It provides self-service visualizations and analytics
- It supports optimization for SAP HANA for the use of detailed data

SAP BusinessObjects Explorer

With SAP BusinessObjects Explorer, we can answer our questions in a very simple way:

- Fast and easy research of data using search
- Easy visualization of data
- Awareness of time and geography
- Usage through mobile access

SAP BusinessObjects Analysis for OLAP

SAP BusinessObjects Analysis allows business analysts to analyze OLAP data in Microsoft Excel and using the web:

- Quick leveraging of existing SAP investments with support for SAP BW and SAP HANA
- Preferred for OLAP analysis conditions
- Highly productive for analysts who use web interfaces

SAP BusinessObjects Predictive Analytics

SAP BusinessObjects Predictive Analytics supplies algorithms to help organizations to gain insights into their organization:

- Statistical analyses of data to understand trends and detect outliers
- A wide range of connectivity to access almost any data
- Helps in showing the future analysis or forecast from models that are put in different conditions

Dashboards and applications

The following are the functions and components of dashboards and applications:

- Build the best visuals for the best user experience
- Build workflows to facilitate the use of custom code
- Navigate and innovate with a rich set of controls such as buttons, list boxes, menus, tabs, and charts

The portfolio comprises the following:

- SAP BusinessObjects Design Studio
- SAP BusinessObjects Dashboards (formerly SAP BusinessObjects Xcelsius Enterprise)

SAP BusinessObjects Design Studio

SAP Business Objects Design Studio is preferred by users when SAP HANA and SAP BW models and engine capabilities are required. It contains a library with a rich set of controls to develop applications for analysis on SAP and HANA:

- Modern development environment and HTML5 runtime
- Native SAP BW and SAP HANA support
- Recommended solution for SAP BW customers (especially those with SAP BEx WAD investments)
- Facilitates pre-built templates with guided procedures to faster design
- Consumes KPIs directly from SAP HANA, semantic layers, and SAP BW
- Flexible SDK to customize visualization, dashboards, and apps
- Facilitates re-usability of queries, InfoCubes, SAP HANA, and other data models/data marts
- Eclipse-based design environment that's easy to scale

SAP BusinessObjects dashboards

SAP BusinessObjects dashboards provides a rich set of visualizations and controls. You can do the following:

- Leverage enterprise BI infrastructure (semantic layer)
- Create dashboards that are highly interactive and display other data sources
- Use a wide range of visualization libraries that support KPIs and executive dashboards

Reporting in the BI platform

The following are the functions and components of reporting:

- Its allows users to create and share information:
    - Easy and rapid construction of formatted reports
    - Distributes reports securely (internally and externally)
    - Reduced IT support cost as it allows end users to create and modify their own reports with ease

- The portfolio contains the following:
    - SAP Crystal Reports
    - SAP BusinessObjects Web Intelligence

Reporting features include the following:

- SAP BusinessObjects Web Intelligence provides self-service reporting whenever necessary or required
- The SAP Crystal Reports SDK provides depth and the ability to embed SAP Crystal Reports
- Ability to access the tools everywhere using mobile, web-based, and desktop access, both online and offline

SAP BusinessObject Web Intelligence

SAP BusinessObject Web Intelligence lets users define their own queries and reporting:

- Quick construction of necessary queries and reports, without any prior experience or knowledge of SQL
- It provides the ability to access tools everywhere using mobile, web-based, and desktop access, both online and offline

SAP Crystal Reports

SAP Crystal Reports allows users to define reports that are well formatted for printing and operational reporting:

- Allows access to almost any data source directly
- Construction of reports that look professional, using pixel-perfect positioning, layout, and templates
- Powerful API used to embed reports into applications
- Optimization possible for high-volume reporting and publishing material

Universal semantic layer

The universal semantic layer is an abstraction layer between the database and the business user. It has the following components:

- Universes
- Query generation
- Calculator
- Local cache
- Query panel
- Database connectivity parameters

The semantic layer hides the complexity of the data structure, and business users do not need to remember any technical names to access it. It allows users to interact with and analyze data regardless of the underlying data sources and schema. It has a collection of the following metadata objects:

- Dimensions
- Measures
- Hierarchies
- Attributes
- Pre-defined calculations
- Functions
- Queries

SAP BusinessObject has two types of Universe: multi-source-enabled relational Universes and dimensional Universes.

With a multi-source-enabled relational Universe, you can access all the major relational sources:

- General access can be enabled with **Open Database Connectivity (ODBC)**
- It supports OLAP sources and SAP BW
- Reduced maintenance, with the use of one optimized source of data and metadata for multiple reports
- Better security and access control of data and who can access what

Benefits of business views

Business views simplify report creation and interaction. A business view supports in the following ways:

- It is specifically created to make an access to data easy, and view-time security for SAP Crystal Report creation
- In a single view, you can combine multiple data sources
- With business views, we can extract company data for report development
- Business views are fully supported in the BI platform

Business views can only be used by SAP Crystal Reports.

Overview of the BI platform suite

The BI platform is a reliable solution for delivering interactive reports to end users. This is done through applications, whether they run from the intranet, extranet, internet, or corporate portal. The BI platform can be installed on a single machine or over a network. Let's take a look at the integration of the BI platform with a customer's existing infrastructure and systems:

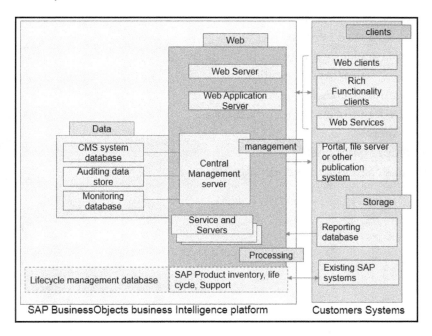

The following server components are installed:

- Platform services
- Connection services
- Data federator services
- SAP Crystal Reports services
- Web Intelligence services
- Dashboard services
- Mobile services
- Life cycle management

The following third-party components are installed:

- Tomcat 8.0 or later
- Subversion

The following client tools are installed:

- **Web Intelligence Rich Client (WRC)**
- **Business View Manager (BVM)**
- Report Conversion Tool
- Universe Design Tool
- Query as a Web Service
- Information Design Tool
- Universe Landscape Migration
- Translation Manager
- Data Federation Administration Tool
- BI Widgets
- Developer components
- Database access and security figure

Client-tier components for integration

The following are the client-tier components for integration:

- **SAP BusinessObjects Analysis for Microsoft Office**: This is a plug-in that is integrated into Microsoft Excel and Microsoft PowerPoint to be used as an OLAP tool. It allows users to get together information from different systems within a single workspace.
- **SAP BusinessObjects Analysis for OLAP**: This is also an OLAP tool (formerly called **voyager**) and it works with multi-dimensional data. Like SAP BusinessObjects Analysis for Microsoft Office, this also allows users to get together information from different systems within a single workspace.
- **SAP Crystal Reports for Enterprise:** SAP Crystal Reports for Enterprise is a design tool that is based on the Java platform. It enables the user to create complex reports in the BI platform.
- **Data Federation Administration Tool:** This enables multi-source Universes by distributing queries across data sources and lets our federated data through a single data foundation. This is a very handy tool for administrators optimizing data federation queries and fine-tuning the data federation query engine for the best possible performance.

Information Design Tool

Information Design Tool (IDT) is mainly used by designers to extract, define, and manipulate metadata from relational and OLAP sources to create and deploy Universes:

- **Life Cycle Management console (web client)**: LCM provides centralized views for monitoring the progress of the entire life cycle process. It is also used to move content from one BI platform to another (same version).
- **Repository Diagnostic Tool (RDT)**: RDT scans, diagnoses, and repairs inconsistencies that might occur between a CMS system database and an FRS file store. It keep tracks of (and reports) repairs and actions that have been completed.

- **Translation Management Tool**: This tool defines multi-lingual Universes and manages translations of Universes and their Web Intelligence documents and prompts.
- **Upgrade Management Tool**: This is mainly used by the administrator to import users, groups, and folders from previous versions of the BI platform. It can import and upgrade objects, events, server groups, repository objects, and calendars.

Data-tier components for integration

The following are data-tier components for integration:

- **Monitoring database**: This is used to store system configuration and component information that is used for SAP support. It is the default monitoring database with an embedded Apache Derby database, which uses the Apache Derby JDBC driver. From SAP BI 4.0 SP4 onward, you can move the monitoring database from the Derby database to the audit database.
- **Universes**: The Universe is the semantic layer between the end user and organizational database. They are built by IDT and can be identified by the `.unx` file extension.

Processing-tier components for integration

The following are the processing-tier components for integration:

- **Adaptive Job Server**: This is used to process and host scheduled jobs for a variety of object types. With default settings, the installation program installs one Adaptive Job Server per host. In many cases (depending on features installed), Adaptive Job Server can also include services such as promotion management, publishing services, and monitoring services.
- **Adaptive Processing Server**: As the name suggests, this is a generic server that takes care of hosting services that are responsible for processing requests for a variety of sources.

- **Connection Server 32**: The SAP BusinessObjects BI 4.x platform is a 64-bit architecture, but we do have 32-bit sources (such as data sources) in the landscape. It allows a connection to be 32 bit .
- **SAP Crystal Reports Processing Server:** This handles the on-demand processing of reports that have been written in any version of Crystal except Crystal for Enterprise. It works in collaboration with SAP Crystal Reports Cache Server. It retrieves data for the requested report from the latest instance (or directly from the data source), converts it into **Encapsulated Page Format** (**EPF**), and then sends it to SAP Crystal Reports Cache Server. EPF returns only the requested page on demand, thereby resulting in high performance and improved throughput.
- **Dashboard Analytics Server**: These are servers used by the BI workspace to create and manage corporate and personal BI workspace module content.
- **Dashboard Design Processing Server:** This is specifically used to respond to requests from the dashboard and process the results.
- **Dashboard Server:** This is used by the BI workspace to create and manage corporate and personal dashboards in the SAP BusinessObjects BI platform.

Storage, management, and web-tier components for integration

The following are the storage, management, and web-tier components for integration:

- **Dashboard Design Cache Server**: This server determines whether a previously served dashboard viewing request would satisfy the current dashboard viewing request. It will attempt to share the previous data results held in its cache. It forwards any request to the processing server if it is unable to complete the request.

- **CMS**: This is a process running as part of BusinessObjects Enterprise Server, which includes a CMS database, authentication, and user audit actions. All of the services on the SAP businessObjects BI platform are managed by CMS, including the access to system files where documents are stored, including user audit information. It is a central service.
- **Web applications:** These run on the web application server and process requests for the web client. The applications consist of the following:
  - **Central Management Console (CMC)**
  - LMC
  - BI launch pad and BI workspaces
  - Web Intelligence Explorer
  - SAP BusinessObjects Analysis for OLAP

SAP BusinessObjects platform – a tool for integration

SAP BusinessObjects comprises multiple tools that support integration. The idea is also to have re-usability and seamless integration of capabilities of the BusinessObjects applications developed on the SAP BusinessObjects BI platform. The following details tools that provide features for integration to SAP BusinessObjects 4.2.

Web interfaces

In this category, we have CMC and the BI launch pad as the main tool. Let's see them in more detail:

- **CMC**: This is a web-based tool that offers a single interface with which we can perform most of the daily administrative tasks (such as user management, content management, and server management). In the following screenshot, we can see the overview of the home page of CMC:

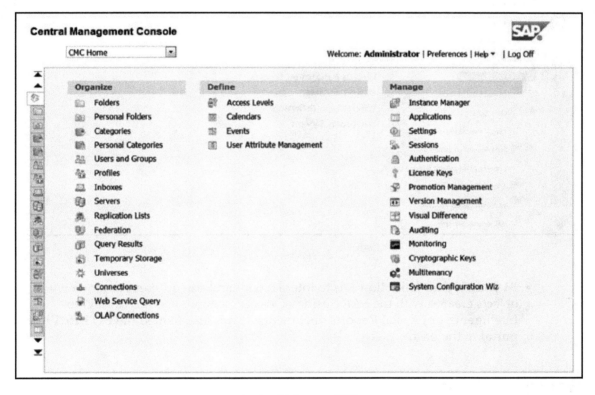

Overview of the home page of CMC

In the following screenshot, we can see the CMS server page:

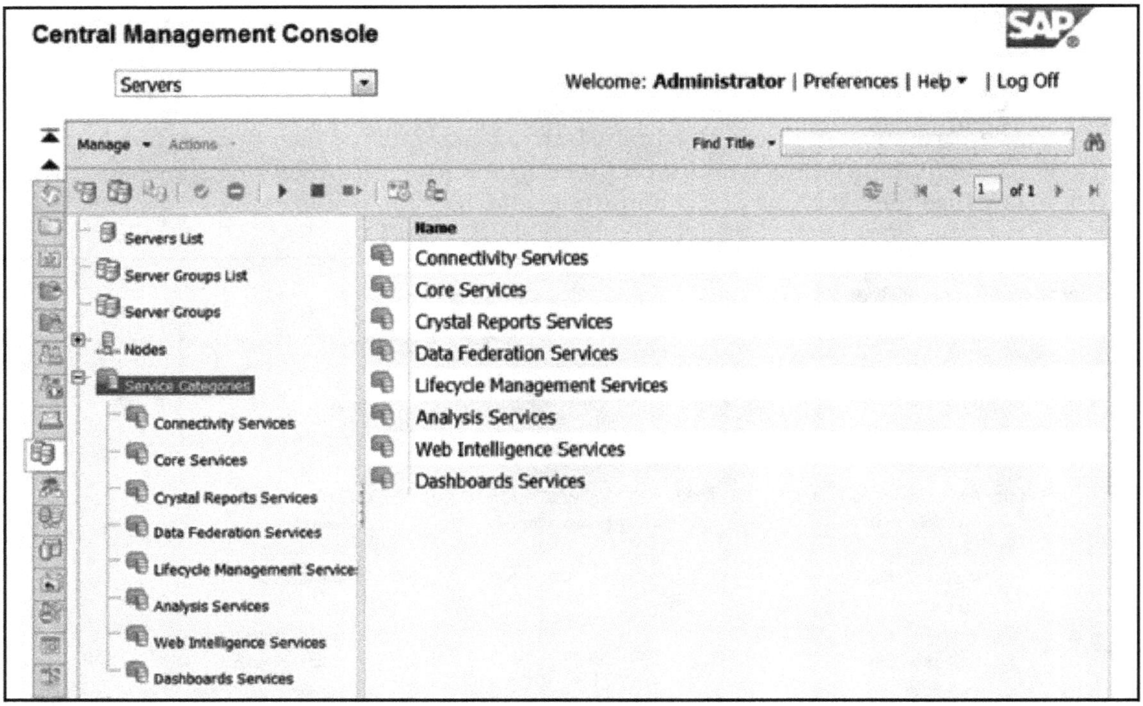

Overview of the CMC server page

- **BI launch pad:** This allows us to interact with and use different deployment objects created with the SAP BusinessObjects components, such as a Web Intelligence or Crystal Reports documents. It was also named the **BO InfoView portal** in the past.

Semantic layer

With a semantic layer in place, you can have a common user experience even when accessing various data sources. Also, the end user or the business user can manipulate the business terms without having to think about the data sources related technical details. We have the following options in the semantic layer:

- **UNX:** A Universe is a semantic layer that maps complex data into descriptive business terms used across the organization. It models data into a shared object model.

- **Multi-source Universes**: These can get together and merge data from SAP BW with other relational databases, such as Oracle and SQL Server. We should make sure that we have selected the **Multisource-Enabled** checkbox as shown in the following screenshot:

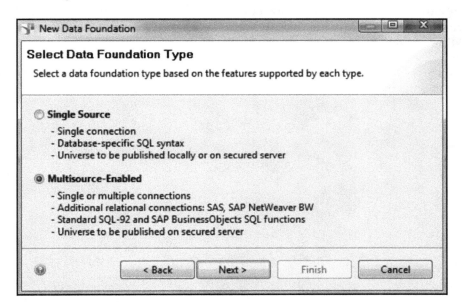

Report content types

Depending on the kind of report required, we can use one of a couple of report content types:

- SAP Crystal Reports
- Web Intelligence

Web Intelligence reports can export tabbed worksheets to Excel, whereas Crystal can't. Web Intelligence requires reporting from Universes; it can't report directly from a database.

Summary

This was the last chapter of this book. With this chapter, we got a general overview of the SAP BusinessObjects BI platform architecture, various BI systems, and the elements contained within those BI systems. It also described the deployment strategy and factors that should be considered during deployment. We learned about the deployment and configuration of SAP BusinessObjects 4.2.

This brings us to the end of this book. We hope you all enjoyed reading it and learned about the concepts of SAP BI.

Other Books You May Enjoy

If you enjoyed this book, you may be interested in these other books by Packt:

Mastering Microsoft Power BI
Brett Powell

ISBN: 9781788297233

- Build efficient data retrieval and transformation processes with the Power Query M Language
- Design scalable, user-friendly DirectQuery and Import Data Models
- Develop visually rich, immersive, and interactive reports and dashboards
- Maintain version control and stage deployments across development, test, and production environments
- Manage and monitor the Power BI Service and the On-Premises Data Gateway
- Develop a fully On-Premise Solution with the Power BI Report Server
- Scale up a Power BI solution via Power BI Premium capacity and migration to Azure Analysis Services or SQL Server Analysis Services

Tableau 2019.x Cookbook
Dmitry Anoshin, Teodora Matic, Slaven Bogdanovic, Tania Lincoln, and Dmitrii Shirokov

ISBN: 9781789533385

- Understand the basic and advanced skills of Tableau Desktop
- Implement best practices of visualization, dashboard, and storytelling
- Learn advanced analytics with the use of build in statistics
- Deploy the multi-node server on Linux and Windows
- Use Tableau with big data sources such as Hadoop, Athena, and Spectrum
- Cover Tableau built-in functions for forecasting using R packages
- Combine, shape, and clean data for analysis using Tableau Prep
- Extend Tableau's functionalities with REST API and R/Python

Leave a review - let other readers know what you think

Please share your thoughts on this book with others by leaving a review on the site that you bought it from. If you purchased the book from Amazon, please leave us an honest review on this book's Amazon page. This is vital so that other potential readers can see and use your unbiased opinion to make purchasing decisions, we can understand what our customers think about our products, and our authors can see your feedback on the title that they have worked with Packt to create. It will only take a few minutes of your time, but is valuable to other potential customers, our authors, and Packt. Thank you!

Index

presentation, creating with BusinessObjects
   Analysis 53
Microsoft
   SAP BusinessObjects Analysis 31
mobile category
   corporate category 209
   personal category 209

O

Online Analytical Processing (OLAP) 31, 74
Open Data Protocol (OData) 220
Open Database Connectivity (ODBC) 230
options, SAP BusinessObjects BI4 deployment
   Amazon Web Services 218
   SAP HANA Enterprise Cloud 218
   SAP hosting partners 218

P

Predictive Analysis Library (PAL) 183
predictive analysis
   forecast 149
   linear regression 149
Predictive Confidence (KR) 186
Predictive Power (KI) 186
Prepare view, SAP Lumira
   about 141
   cleaning panel 143
   column data manipulation panel 142
   data editing panel 143
   data manipulation panel 142
   data panel 141
   Object Picker 142
presentation, creating with BusinessObjects
   Analysis
   creating with analysis for PowerPoint based on
     SAP BW data 59, 61, 63
   creating, for Microsoft PowerPoint 54
   creating, with analysis for PowerPoint 57
   data source, inserting 55
processing-tier components, for integration
   Adaptive Job Server 234
   Adaptive Processing Server 234
   Connection Server 32 234
   Dashboard Analytics Server 235
   Dashboard Design Processing Server 235

Dashboard Server 235
SAP Crystal Reports Processing Server 235

Q

Query Panel
   used, for creating query on Business Layer 24

R

radar chart 101
relational database management system (RDBMS)
   219
rights, BI platforms
   access levels 207
   folder-level security 206
   inheritance 208
   object-level security 205
   top-level folder security 206
RRI
   reference 49

S

SAP Automated Analytics
   classification example 186
   data understanding phase 185
   evaluation phase 185
   features 181, 182
   model performance indicators 186
   modeling phase 185
SAP BI
   applications and dashboards 8
   data discovery 8
   platform, features 9
   reporting 9
SAP Business Explorer (BEx) 31
SAP BusinessObjects 4.2
   components 9
SAP BusinessObjects Analysis
   Combine and Display groups 35
   Data Analysis group 35
   Data Source group 34
   for Microsoft 31, 32
   groups 34
   Insert group 35
   report to report interface 49, 53
   Tools groups 35